100 Inspirational Sayings of Prophet Muhammed ﷺ

A GIFT FOR EVERY HUMAN BEING:

100

Inspirational Sayings of Prophet Muhammed ﷺ

Compilation and Commentary by

NAZIM MANGERA

Introduction and Editing by

CASSANDRA WILLIAMS, ESQ.

First Edition: 2012
Second Reprint: 2013

ISBN-13: 978-0-9883174-0-6

Cover Photo: Mosque where Prophet Muhammed is buried in Madinah, Saudi Arabia

Nazim Mangera
www.inspirational100.org

Distributed in USA by Al-Rashad Books
www.al-rashad.com *Email:* orders@al-rashad.com
(330) 203-1522

Distributed in Canada by Al Zahra Booksellers
www.alzahraonline.com *Email:* info@alzahraonline.com
416-312-7213

Printed and bound in the United States of America

"We did not send you as a Prophet except out of compassion for everything or We did not send you as a Prophet except to be an embodiment of compassion for everything."

[*Quran: 21:107*]

ﷺ : ***Sallallahu Alaihe Wasallam***

The Arabic prayer means "Peace and blessings of God be upon him" and it usually follows Prophet Muhammed's name. It is said by Muslims when Prophet Muhammed's name is heard or mentioned, out of reverence for him.

R.A.: Radhiallahu Anhu or Anha

The Arabic prayer means "May God be pleased with him or her" and is said by Muslims after mentioning any of Prophet Muhammed 's companions out of love for them.

Hadith: Arabic word which means "Saying of Prophet Muhammedﷺ"

To

Prophet Muhammed ﷺ

and every human being
who promulgates peace and love

Contents

Introduction

The gifts of open mindedness, knowledge, understanding and wisdom have in our modern times too often been substituted for narrowness, presumptiveness, bigotry and brashness. Too many generalizations have been accepted as universal truths. Too much hatred has been brewed from the dissemination, both accidental and intentional, of misinformation. Perhaps those most affected by modern-day mudslinging are the billion plus Muslims around the world who have been systematically and ridiculously lumped into a homogeneous box labeled "terrorist" since that fateful September day in 2001.

I took the "shahadah" declaring my intention to commit myself to the Islamic way of life in June of 2001, not even three months before 9/11. Many may have had their faith shaken by the events of that year and what transpired as a result, but because I had been blessed with an open mind and access to resources about my faith to equip me with knowledge, I was able to see past the events of one day and the actions of a few people and see the religion of Islam for exactly what it is—a way of life that aims to perfect its adherents' character and manners in the pursuit of creating a community focused on pleasing the Almighty.

One of the most inspiring and revealing sources of information that I treasure are the hadith (sayings) of the Prophet Muhammad (may the peace and blessings of Allah be with him and his family). These sayings are so valuable to me and should be to Muslims and non-Muslims alike because they reveal the heart and soul of Islam. Further, these sayings are timeless—the lessons they contain are just as relevant today as they were when they were uttered over 1,400 years ago. The emphasis on character development and the adoption of good manners by the Prophet Muhammad (peace be upon him) created the foundation upon which Muslim families and entire societies have flourished, and if followed today, can have the same effect.

Unfortunately, two separate forces have come together to create a perfect storm—the neglect of and failure to learn the traditions of the Prophet (peace be upon him) by many Muslims around the world and simultaneously the mournful failure of some non-Muslims to seek or be given the information about Islam and the Prophet (peace be upon him) before vitriolic opinions have been formed and fortified in the minds of the masses. Both these forces have led us to where we are today, a wary and unstable peace hangs in the balance between Muslims and non-Muslims around the globe, for no justifiable reason.

To hurdle these boundaries we have erected between us, we as Muslims must be patient, be willing to work hard to share our knowledge and most importantly, start walking the talk. This book, A Gift for Every Human Being: 100 Inspirational Sayings of Prophet Muhammed ﷺ, is a perfect example of just the type of resource we as Muslims should be focused on providing, especially for non-Muslims who will benefit greatly from the in-depth look into the mind and heart of the Prophet (peace be upon him) as he guides his community toward personal, familial and social bliss and harmony with the Creator.

It was not only an absolute joy and honor to help Nazim compile his commentary on these selected hadith, but it was also a reminder with each page I turned, of why I consciously chose to make Islam my way of life. I pray that this book reaches the hands of many of my brothers and sisters in Islam so that they can be reminded of the incredible legacy the Prophet (peace be upon him) left for us to follow. I also pray that this book reaches the hands of many of people who do not claim to follow Islam, but who have an open mind and an open heart to read these sayings and realize the gentleness, sophistication and positive impacts of this religious tradition.

CASSANDRA WILLIAMS, Esq.
California, USA

*Who is Prophet Muhammed*ﷺ*?*

Prophet Muhammedﷺ was born in 570 CE in the blessed Saudi Arabian city of Makkah. Makkah was founded by Prophet Abraham and his son Prophet Ishmael. Fourteen centuries later, Prophet Muhammedﷺ's influence is still felt across the globe and his teachings are appreciated by both Muslims and non-Muslims alike. More than 1.5 billion people worldwide commit to Prophet Muhammedﷺ's teachings. He is extremely beloved to every Muslim and that is why the name Muhammed, with its variations, is probably the most common given name in the world.

Early Life: Muhammedﷺ's father died before his birth. His mother died when he was six and hence, he became fully orphaned at a young age. His grandfather Abdul Muttalib and his uncle Abu Talib raised him. As a young man, Muhammedﷺ enjoyed an esteemed reputation because of his upright character. He was known throughout the city as 'the truthful and the trustworthy.' He worked as a merchant as well as a shepherd and married at the age of 25.

Prophethood: At the age of forty, during one of his spiritual seclusions in a cave on the outskirts of Makkah, angel Gabriel gloriously manifested himself to Muhammedﷺ pronouncing revelation from God. Alarmed and shivering he fled to his wife, begging her to wrap him in a cloak. He feared for his sanity, concerned that a desert spirit might be pursuing him. More revelations soon followed and Muhammedﷺ came to the understanding that he was not only a prophet in a long line of prophets such as Adam, Noah, Abraham, Moses, and Jesus (peace be upon all of them) but that he was the last of them who was sent with a universal message. He continued to receive revelation through Gabriel for many years to come. These revelations came to be known as the Quran, the Muslim divine book.

In Makkah: For thirteen years he invited his clan in Makkah to worship the one God, to respect women as full equals and the source of human mercy, and to care for the widows, the orphans, the weak and the oppressed. At first people ridiculed and feared Muhammedﷺ's message because it threatened their financial gains because pilgrims from all over Arabia came to visit the idols in Makkah, and, consequently, spent their wealth. The ridicule soon turned to oppression, and many of Prophet Muhammedﷺ's followers were tortured and killed. In 615 CE, Muhammedﷺ ordered some of his followers to immigrate to Ethiopia to seek the protection and the shelter of the just Christian Ethiopian king. A few years later his entire clan was excommunicated causing many to starve to death, including his beloved wife Khadijah and his uncle Abu Talib. The Makkahn's ill treatment culminated in an unsuccessful assassination attempt on Prophet Muhammedﷺ's life, after which he was forced to leave the city of his birth and migrate to the enlightened city of Madinah.

To Madinah: The Prophet then moved to Madinah, where he established an unprecedented peace between the city's two largest tribes who had been suffering from feudal wars for centuries. With Prophet Muhammedﷺ as its leader, the city's virtue was restored and the population began to prosper once again. He also secured the rights of the Jewish minority by granting them full citizenship and freedom to practice their religion without constraint. The peace the Muslims enjoyed in Madina would not be long-lived. Even while exiled, the Makkahn's continued their attempts to undermine Prophet Muhammedﷺ. The Prophet's growing influence was a threat to their dominance in Arabia. After successfully establishing a stable community, God told the Prophet through revelation that he and his community could now defend themselves. In battle against the merciless and tyrannical, he was as courageous as a great lion; and with the weak and oppressed, he was as gentle as a shepherd.

Return to Makkah: After several large battles, the Muslims and the Makkahn's established a treaty, which was violated by the Makkahn's only two years later. The Prophet then gathered an army of ten thousand soldiers and marched upon Makkah, conquering it without bloodshed. After suffering twenty bitter years at the hands of the Makkahn's, in which he lost his wife, uncle, and several other companions, Muhammed ﷺ was now in a position of complete control. The Makkahn's were at his mercy; and mercy they were given. The Prophet Muhammed told the Makkahn's that they were free and would suffer no harm. He said to them, "This is the day of mercy." Prophet Muhammed ﷺ passed away in 632 CE and is buried in Madinah, Saudi Arabia.

Mercy to the World: In twenty-three short years, Prophet Muhammed ﷺ spread monotheism throughout the peninsula, unified warring tribes, taught the honor of women, and established that all people were equal in the sight of God. He elevated the low and lowered the arrogant that they might meet in that middle place known as brotherhood. He infused within people a love of learning unleashing a creative power that would lead to some of the most extraordinary scientific breakthroughs in human history. The Prophet Muhammed ﷺ's entire life, up until his last breath, was spent in the liberation of others. He liberated people from misguidance, oppression, and greed. Even on his deathbed, his last words were, "Treat your women well, and do not oppress your servants..." The world needs a deeper understanding of this man—his gentleness towards children, his love of animals, his concern for the weak and oppressed, and his sense of justice always tempered with mercy. He taught us that forbearance is greater than revenge; forgiveness more lofty than punishment; and compassion more effective than austerity. Above all, he taught us mercy. And in these difficult times, we are all in need of more mercy in the world.

[With editing from:
http://www.celebratemercy.com/AboutMuhammad.aspx]

My Chain of Transmission

A prophetic statement consists of two aspects: The text of the report (Arabic: Matn) containing the actual narrative; and the chain of narrators (Arabic: Isnad or Sanad) which documents the route by which the report has been transmitted. The Sanad consists of a chain of the transmitters each mentioning the name of the person from whom they heard the prophetic statement until mentioning the originator of the matn along with the matn itself.

The Isnad precedes the actual text (*matn*) and looks like the following: "It has been related to me by A on the authority of B on the authority of C on the authority of D (usually a Companion of the Prophet) that Prophet Muhammed ﷺ said..."

Isnad is a unique feature of the religion of Islam. Early Muslim scholars examined and analyzed each and every statement that came to them, whether it was the statement of Prophet Muhammed ﷺ, his companions or anyone else. They studied the life and character, in the strictest way possible, of those who were part of the transmitting chain (Isnad).

Thus, Muslims witnessed an amazing introduction of the science of studying the reporters of Hadith which was unprecedented and is unrivalled. The recording of the names, dates of demise, qualities and characteristics of thousands and thousands of people is something that is unique to Islam.

"Dr. Aloys Sprenger (1813-1893), the celebrated Austrian scholar, acknowledged in his introduction to the Isabah the unsurpassable feat of Muslim historiography in these words:

> 'The glory of the literature of the Mohammedans is its literary biography. There is no nation, nor has there been any which like them has during twelve centuries recorded the life of every man of letters. If the biographical records of the Mohammedans were collected, we should probably have accounts of the lives of half a million of distinguished persons, and it would be

found that there is not a decennium of their history, nor a place of importance which has not its representatives.'" [Page #40, Muhammad: The Ideal Prophet, Sulayman Nadwi (d.1953)]

The following is my Isnad till Prophet Muhammed ﷺ of the first prophetic statement in Bukhari:

1. Nazim Mangera
2. *I narrate from my beloved teacher:* Shaykh Muhammed Izharul Hasan Kandhalwi (birth: **November 03, 1919,** death: **9:30 AM, Tuesday, August 13, 1996)** He passed away in Nizamuddin, New Delhi, India, and I was present there on that day. It was one of the saddest days of my life.
3. *Who narrates from:* Shaykulhadith Zakariyya Kandhalwi (b.1898, d.1982)
4. *Who narrates from:* Khalil Ahmed Saharanpuri (b.1852, d.1927)
5. *Who narrates from:* Shah Abdul Ghani Dehlawi (b.1819, d.1878)
6. *Who narrates from:* Shah Muhammad Ishaq Dehlawi (b.1783, d.1846)
7. *Who narrates from:* Shah Abdul Aziz Dehlawi (b.1746, d.1823)
8. *Who narrates from:* Shah Waliyullah Dehlawi (b.1702, d.1760)
9. *Who narrates from:* Abu Tahir Kurdi (b.1670, d.1732)
10. *Who narrates from his father:* Ibrahim Kurdi (b.1616, d.1689)
11. *Who narrates from:* Ahmad al Qushashi (d.1660)
12. *Who narrates from:* Ahmad ibn Quoddous Shinnawi (b.1567, d.1618)
13. *Who narrates from:* Shams ad Din Ramli (b.1513, d.1595)
14. *Who narrates from:* Zainu'd-Din Zakariyya Ansari (b.1420, d.1520)
15. *Who narrates from:* Hafidh ibn Hajar Asqalani (b.1371, d.1448)
16. *Who narrates from:* Ibrahim ibn Ahmad Tanukhi (b.1309, d.1397)
17. *Who narrates from:* Ahmad ibn Talib Hajjar (b.1226, d.1329)
18. *Who narrates from:* Siraj Hussain ibn Mubarak Zabidi (b.1151, d.1233)
19. *Who narrates from:* Abdul Awwal ibn Isa Harawi (b.1065, d.1158)
20. *Who narrates from:* Abdur Rahman ibn Muzaffar Dawoodi (b.984, d.1074)

21. *Who narrates from:* Abu Muhammad Abdululllah Sarakhsi (b.905, d.991)
22. *Who narrates from:* Muhammad ibn Yusuf Farbari (b.845, d.932)
23. *Who narrates from:* Muhammad ibn Ismail Al Bukhari (b.809, d.869)
24. *Who narrates from:* Humaydi Abdullah Ibn Zubair (d.834)
25. *Who narrates from:* Sufyan ibn Uyaynah (b.725, d.815)
26. *Who narrates from:* Yahya ibn Saeed Ansari (d.761)
27. *Who narrates from:* Muhammad ibn Ibrahim Taime (b.666, d.737)
28. *Who narrates from:* Alqama ibn Waqqas Laythi (d. 689)
29. *Who narrates from:* Umar ibnul Khattab (b.581, d.644)
30. *Who narrates from:* Prophet Muhammed ﷺ (b.570, d.632)

Who said, "Actions will be rewarded according to intentions." (Bukhari)

The above chain of transmission is so inspiring and every time I read it, I feel so honoured to be a part of that chain of transmission! You will notice that some narrators were very young when they heard the above prophetic statement. But that is not surprising because the Hadith books were already compiled by then. Also, I know a Muslim boy in Toronto, Canada, who memorized the full Quran from cover to cover by the tender age of seven. So there is no need to be surprised if some of the above narrators were very young when their teachers passed away.

The younger the transmitters, the shorter the chain is to Prophet Muhammed ﷺ. Islamic scholars have discussed about the minimum age requirement for the transmitters of Hadith. Since, the discussion is not relevant to this book, I will leave it out.

I have not seen the Isnad compiled like the above, with the dates, in the English language, or as a matter of fact in any other language. I am happy that I am the first person to compile it in such a unique manner.

Preface

"By speech first, but far more by writing, man has been able to put something of himself beyond death. In tradition and in books an integral part of the individual persists, for it can influence the minds and actions of other people in different places and at different times: a row of black marks on a page can move a man to tears, though the bones of him that wrote it are long ago crumbled to dust." *Julian Huxley (1887-1975)*

After sifting through countless books, going over 1000's of Hadiths, and putting the final ones through the process of elimination, I finally chose the 100 which you have in your hands right now. But that was the easy part; the hard part was putting together this book. Through this two year long process (which included writing in three different countries and many airplanes and airport lounges), many people have played an instrumental part in compiling this book and it would be an act of ungratefulness if I did not thank them. I would first of all like to thank Allah for granting me the opportunity to put this book together. I would also like to acknowledge the help of the following amazing people:

1. Mark Woloszyn of Amherst, NY, USA: Mark, you were the first person I sought feedback from about this type of book and its usefulness for Muslims and non-Muslims alike. Your initial encouragement made it possible for me to complete this book. Thanks for the feedback on my initial compilation and the time you spent in going over them with me.
2. Cassandra Williams of California, USA and Dubai, UAE: I will never be able to thank you enough for the countless hours you put in to edit the book and for writing the wonderful introduction to the book. You spent time throughout your pregnancy and even found time for this book after delivering your beautiful son Zackariyah. Your son will be extremely proud to have an inspiring mom like you! Even though I have never met you, and I only

became acquainted with you and corresponded with you through the internet after reading your inspiring articles, I'm sure you inspire everyone around you with your attention to detail.

3. Suleman Din also in Dubai, UAE and Toronto, Canada: I am particularly grateful to you for volunteering to meticulously review the 100 and for offering invaluable editorial advice. For the valuable suggestion about the book cover, you deserve from me a cup of hot chocolate from Tim Hortons. If I ever come to Dubai, take me to a Timmies and the bill is on me.
4. My wife, Sawdah, and my three beautiful children Rayhan, Kulthoom, and Yusuf: I can never thank you all enough for filling my life with so much happiness and laughter which stimulated me to progress at a steady pace till I finished this book! Kulthoom, thank you for showing so much excitement when I told you about this book! Yusuf, what can I say to you since you are only 3 years old. Yusuf, you sure were a handful! Yusuf, I did not appreciate you making life difficult for me because of pulling out so many keys from our laptop keyboard and forcing me to use it without some of the keys! To all of you, I apologize for not being with you as much as I would have liked to.
5. Muhammad Chothia (my brother-in-law) in Trinidad and originally from Barbados: I appreciated your quick assistance with the compilation of my Isnad (chain of transmission) and for being so diligent with the dates.

May Allah perpetually reward you all and the many others who helped throughout the different stages in the completion of this book.

And lastly, I would like to thank all those non-Muslims who I met at many interfaith events for motivating me to write this book because of them asking me if a book like this exists or not. The most recent question I had about this type of book was on June 17th, 2012, at the Unitarian Universalist Church in Hamburg, NY.

Every time I read the 100, I am inspired by them. I hope you are inspired by them as well. If you have any comments or criticisms about the book, please do contact me through the below mentioned website.

NAZIM MANGERA
Amherst, New York
Friday, September 28, 2012
www.inspirational100.org

THE 100

Kind Treatment of Non-Muslims

1. Asma bint Abu Bakr (R.A.) reports that she came to Prophet Muhammed ﷺ and said, "O Messenger of God! My mother, who is a non-Muslim, has come to visit me and she desires to be close to me and to give me gifts. Shall I greet her and treat her well?" Prophet Muhammed ﷺ replied, "Greet your (non-Muslim) mother and treat her well." [Bukhari]

Commentary: Though her mother is a non-Muslim, the Muslim child is still advised to be kind and respectful towards her. No matter what faith your parents belong to, in Islam, respecting your parents is of paramount importance. The Hadith also teaches us (1) to offer kindness to others, regardless of their religious leaning, (2) to offer kindness to our parents especially, and (3) that fraternizing with non-Muslims is permissible for Muslims.

2. Prophet Muhammed ﷺ said, "I am nearest to the son of Mary (Jesus) in this world and in the hereafter." [Bukhari]

Commentary: The statement informs us how revered Prophet Jesus (peace be upon him) was to Prophet Muhammed ﷺ. It is the belief of the Muslims that the next and the final Prophet after Prophet Jesus (peace be upon him) was Prophet Muhammed ﷺ. There is a span of nearly 600 years between the two illustrious prophets. I visited the country of Panama a couple of years ago. As I was leaving a store, the store owner, whilst pointing towards me said something in Spanish to my relative. I asked him what she said. He replied that she said that I look like Prophet Jesus.

3. Prophet Muhammed ﷺ said, "No one has permission to leave out three things: 1) To be kind to parents, whether they are Muslim or non-Muslim 2) To fulfill a promise, whether it is for a Muslim or a non-Muslim 3) To return a thing kept in trust to its owner, whether the owner is a Muslim or a non-Muslim." [IbnAsakir, Jaame-us-Saghir]

Commentary: Many misconceptions exist with regard to the interactions between Muslims and those who do not follow the Islamic faith. Some of these misconceptions have arisen out of either intentional or accidental misreading of Qur'anic texts taken out of context. Other misconceptions have arisen because Muslims themselves have acted in ways, claiming to represent Islam or under the banner of Islam, which are blatantly contrary to actual Islamic teachings regarding Muslim/Non-Muslim interactions. These misconceptions usually involve the idea that Muslims are divinely ordered to be harsh or to be deceptive with non-Muslims. As the above statement makes clear, it is imperative for every Muslim to act kindly, honestly, and honorably with everyone regardless of their religious leanings.

[God does not forbid you from dealing kindly and justly with those who do not fight you because of faith nor drive you out of your homes, for God loves those who are just.] [Quran-60:8]

4. A funeral procession once passed in front of Prophet Muhammed ﷺ and he stood up. It was said to him that it was a coffin of a Jewish person. He said, "Is the deceased not a human?" [Bukhari]

Commentary: Irrespective of a person's beliefs, since we are all human beings and share a common ancestry, Prophet Adam and his wife, Eve, we should show decency to one another. The differences in faith, color, race, language, nationality do not take away from our common humanity and hence all human beings deserve our respect.

When Prophet Muhammed ﷺ died, his armor was placed as collateral with a Jewish person for some amounts of barley, which proves that he had financial dealings with non-Muslims until he passed away. It was never his desire to harm or hurt any non-Muslim just because of their beliefs.

5. Prophet Muhammed ﷺ was requested, "Messenger of God, invoke a curse on the idolaters." He ﷺ replied, "I have not been sent as a Prophet to curse anyone but rather, I was sent as a cause of mercy." [Muslim]

Commentary: This is one of the most powerful narrations of an interaction of Prophet Muhammed ﷺ, both on a superficial level regarding the actual situation of the hadith and on a universal level regarding the general character and mission of the Prophet. In this exchange, the Prophet is requested to curse the idolaters, the very people his message is intended to change, and the people that often would prove to be the most oppressive toward the Prophet and his followers. Despite the friction between those who stubbornly resisted the message of the Prophet and those who accepted Islam, the Prophet refused to treat the idolaters with brutality or disdain. His attitude was one much more fueled by hope of future change than one powered by anger or impatience.

The Prophet understood his role as a messenger of God's mercy, and hence, through his interactions, he exemplified mercy. His mercy, however, was imbued with fortitude, so the Prophet struck a perfect balance between strength and sensitivity. There are stories of the Prophet shortening the congregational prayers if he heard a baby crying and in need of his mother's assistance. Other traditions tell us of the Prophet's kind dealings with animals, his playfulness and generosity with young children, and his tenderness and respect toward women. And there are scores of stories of the Prophet's forgiveness and mercy shown to his enemies and detractors. This hadith is just another example of why the Prophet Muhammed ﷺ has been called a "mercy to mankind."

Once again, the beautiful teachings of an amazing person come through with an emphatic lesson for Muslims of being respectful towards non-Muslims. He is reminding all of us that he was sent as a mercy and a source of peace and tranquility for all human beings. The obvious corollary of implementing his teachings will be that all of us will be blessed with a life of happiness and tranquility.

Parents

6. Prophet Muhammed ﷺ said, "No parent can give a better gift to their child than good manners." [Tirmidhi]

Commentary: This hadith is a piece of wisdom for all times and for all people—it is truly universal. As we have "progressed" as a society, so too have we regressed in our manners and etiquette. That is not to say that it is necessary for us to revert back to any particular set of mannerisms, but rather to highlight the lack of emphasis we put on manners in our modern culture and the observable need for us to implement some sort of propriety in our children so that we can advance our civilization.

It is the responsibility of the parents to make sure that they teach their children good manners, sound morals, and demonstrate noble values. It is our duty as parents to guide the future of humanity by teaching our children to respect everyone and everything around them. Bearing children is a daunting task (and the highest levels of respect should be given to women who carry children in their womb and bear them), but what is critically important is that parents fulfill the responsibility to impart good manners onto their children so that they are stewards of this world. The home is the first environment in which our children grow, and where their inclinations, attitudes and personalities are formed. This explains the importance of the parents' role in nurturing their young ones and paying equal attention to their physical, mental and spiritual wellbeing. Not only is the imparting of good manners an important role for parents, but it is also a gift that they give to their children, and it would be wise of children to think of these lessons as gifts rather than as irritations. Prophet Muhammad ﷺ called good manners gifts because of the benefits they reap those who obtain them throughout their lives.

7. Once a man came to Prophet Muhammed ﷺ and asked, "O Messenger of God, which person of all the people is best entitled to kind treatment and good companionship from me?" He answered, "Your mother." The man asked, "And then?" He said, "Your mother." The man asked again, "And after her?" He said, "Your mother." The man asked for a fourth time, "And after her?" Prophet Muhammed ﷺ said, "Your father." [Bukhari]

Commentary: This hadith should serve to dispel the notion that, God forbid, the religion of Islam or Prophet Muhammad ﷺ taught anything but the utmost respect for women, particularly for mothers. The Prophet recognized the partnership of the mother and father in the raising of children, but also refused to ignore the special and unique role of a mother in the life of her child. Mothers endure hardship through pregnancy and hardship through childbirth that fathers never experience. Further, most mothers endure hardship through the day to day raising of children that most fathers are not involved with. Hence, according to the hadith, mothers are given respect and honor to a degree higher than fathers because of these extra efforts they endure. This statement teaches us that the person most deserving to be shown kindness is a mother. Mothers endure hardships for children on three different occasions: during pregnancy, at the time of delivery of the child, and while she raises the child. These hardships that the mother goes through is much more than what any father will ever go through to bring up children. Both parents must be respected at all times, but our mother is more deserving of our respect. Both parents must be respected at all times, but our mothers are given preference because of the physical difficulties she undergoes during the various stages of her child's life.

8. Prophet Muhammed ﷺ said, "The happiness of God lies in the happiness of the parent and the displeasure of God lies in the displeasure of the parent." [Tirmidhi]

Commentary: The modern social structures that have taken over the minds of us today do not include the level of kindness and respect towards parents that most deserve or the concept of caring for them in their old age and protecting them from neglect in their later years. As we grow, we are taught to be self-sufficient and selfish, to not have time, money or resources to give our parents their due when they are in need. We often think in a "what have you done for me lately" mentality when it comes to our parents instead of a "what can I do for you?" mentality, without realizing the wisdom, the memories, and the goodness we could reap by showing kindness and mercy toward our parents as they age.

This hadith is not only a statement for adult children to think about but also for young children to think about. A child's treatment of his or her parents is a reflection of his or her treatment of God. Our parents are those we owe the most to, those who gave us a chance at life, those who sustain us when we are unable to sustain ourselves, those who make our lives possible and comfortable. While we as children are not to worship our parents, we are to treat them with the utmost respect and honor for the sacrifices they have made for us and the opportunities they provide to us.

The above beautiful statement advises us that if we wish to attain the pleasure of God, then we should strive to please our parents. When our parents reach old age, we need to take extra care of them just as they took extra care of us when we were children. We should provide financial aid to our parents if needed, just as they spent on us. We should treat our parents just like how we would like to be treated by our children. We should never shout, scream, or get angry at our parents.

Taking Care of Daughters

9. **Prophet Muhammed said, "Whoever has a female (daughter) under his guardianship, and he neither buries her alive, nor treats her with contempt, nor gives preference to his sons over her, God will admit him to paradise." [Abu Dawood]**

Commentary: At first glance, this hadith may raise some eyebrows with its mention of burying daughters alive. However, we must read the hadith in its proper historical context. During the life of Prophet Muhammad in Arabia, the birth of a daughter was viewed as a burden on the family, as bad luck, and as a curse from the gods. Many families resorted to burying their newborn daughters alive in order to rid themselves of this perceived burden, bad luck and curse. Taking this historical context into account, this hadith and the overt prohibition of the slaying of children in any way, but particularly of girls in this manner, can be appreciated for its progressive tilt. Honor killings, forced marriages, or repression of women are all cultural aberrations, and are not derived from Islam or the teachings of the Prophet Muhammad in any way, shape or form.

Not only is this hadith overtly progressive for its stance against infanticide, but it goes a step further in its revolutionary spirit. Prophet Muhammad stated that those parents who are entered into paradise will be those who treat their daughters and sons equally, without preference for one over the other. Again, for an era in which females were viewed as nothing but property and burdensome hindrances, this teaching of Prophet Muhammad is nothing short of avant-garde.

Islam has taught the males of this world how important it is for us to respect females, specifically our daughters. Islam ordered men to respect their daughters at a time when daughters were treated with such contempt that they were even buried alive. Sadly, even though the above teachings are more than 1,400 years old, female infanticide and genital mutilation is still widespread in some countries. Fetuses are aborted for no other reason other than for being a female. If a few Muslims mistreat their female family members, the pristine teachings of Islam should not be held responsible. Honor killings, forced marriages, or repression of women's rights are cultural aberrations, not Islamic ones. Throughout his life, Prophet Muhammed ﷺ truly displayed respect to females.

10. Prophet Muhammed ﷺ said, "Shall I show you the greatest form of charity?" He replied, "Yes, indeed, Messenger of God!" He went on, "To provide for your daughter when she is returned to you (after she is divorced or widowed) and there is no one besides you to look after her." [Tirmidhi]

Commentary: Again, at first glance, this hadith may appear to be highlighting a perceived weakness in women. However, on further inspection, the above statement teaches us that if our daughter comes back to live with us for any reason, and we provide financial help to her, then that will be the greatest form of charity. It is considered highly meritorious because of the following reasons: 1) It is considered charity 2) We are helping out someone in their hardship 3) We are looking after our daughter in her greatest moment of need 4) We are maintaining the ties of kinship. The Prophet with his practical advice which recognizes the realities of people's lives in all times and places, recognizes the fact that a daughter may face circumstances in her life which make it necessary or advantageous for her to return to her parents home—sometimes it will be a transition between school and finding a job, other times it will be due to the close of a relationship, and there are definitely other reasons. This hadith offers the parents the comfort that will soothe their troubled spirit and ease any stress they may feel with this added responsibility. The Prophet tells these parents that whatever they spend on their daughter who has come home to them is one of the greatest acts of charity and one of the deeds that will bring them closest to God.

Husband and Wife Relationship

11. Prophet Muhammed ﷺ said, "The best of you are those who are the best to their wives." [Tirmidhi]

Commentary: If we want to be considered to be the best, then we are advised to be the best in our behavior with our wives. Once again, the teachings of Islam have shown the utmost respect to females. The female is respected as a child. She is respected as a daughter. She is respected as a wife. She is respected as a sister. She is respected as a mother. She is respected as an aunt. She is respected as a grandmother. Through its teachings, Islam has provided respect and honor to a female in every single phase of her life! The Prophet gave many recommendations concerning women, to the extent that in the above inspiring statement, the husband who treats his wife well is considered among the best of human beings.

The Prophet was aware of the social phenomenon regarding women—that strong civilizations would result from the raising of strong children by their mothers. Again, this is not to minimize the role of fathers, but only to highlight the insightfulness and perceptive nature of the Prophet when it came to the matter of women and their rights. He understood that giving women their rights and their respect would not only result in a more harmonious society that was conducting itself with dignity, but also that it would result in a society enriched and fortified by women encouraged and emboldened to raise strong, noble, responsible, upright children who would then be ready to carry the torch from generation to generation.

12. Prophet Muhammed ﷺ said, "A believing man must not hate a believing woman. If he dislikes one of her

habits, he will find another habit which will please him." [Muslim]

Commentary: As human beings, we all have good habits and bad habits. But the Prophet of Mercy has advised us to overlook the bad traits of our wives because her good habits outweigh her faults. We have been advised to appreciate each other's good qualities and to forgive each other's shortcomings. If we want happiness in our married life, then we must learn to overlook the weaknesses of our spouse. Every effort should be made to ameliorate and rectify our weaknesses but our spouse must not constantly nag us for shortcomings which no human being is free of. Let us correct our own blemishes and forgive the imperfections of our wife or husband. We foolishly seek perfection in others but we ourselves are not perfect. Once again, the religion of Islam instills in the husband the importance of taking the lead with this issue, forgoing being petty and focusing on small problems or annoyances, being kind and gentle with his spouse.

13. Prophet Muhammed ﷺ said, "Many women have been visiting Muhammed's house complaining about their husbands (that the husbands are beating them). Those who do so (beat their wives) are not the best from among you." [Abu Dawood]

Commentary: We learn from the above statement that the Prophet of Mercy discouraged people from hitting their wives by saying that those who do so are not the best ones. There is further evidence from many other sayings of the Prophet that strictly forbid physical abuse, the hitting of anyone on his or her face, and any physical behavior that leaves any types of marks or scars. The Prophet never hit any female in his life, and he is the ideal role model for every person, particularly every man in his capacity as a husband.

The Prophet was keenly aware of the brutish mentality widespread in the region, and frankly, in the world, at the time of his Prophethood. Unfortunately, while we may decry that mentality outwardly, even in a socially progressive nation like the United States, more than three women are murdered at the hands of their husbands or boyfriends every single day. [http://www.futureswithoutviolence.org/content/action_center/detail/754]

The Prophet was also a gentle man, and an intelligent man, who understood that physical abuse never resulted in anything beneficial. Resentment, mental and emotional damage, health problems, jealousy, disloyalty, etc. were the results of physical abuse, whereas, those who could control their anger and solve their problems amicably and with dignity would not only develop superior social skills, but they would also gain the respect and honor of their family members, their community, and the world. So this direction from the Prophet was not only one meant to soothe domestic tensions and set ground rules for how spouses should interact with one another, but it was also a broader lesson for every person to take heed that controlling anger is always the prescription for a better result.

14. Prophet Muhammed ﷺ said, "Every one of you is responsible and each of you will be questioned about those under his supervision. A ruler is responsible and he will be questioned about those in his care. A man is a guardian of his family and is responsible for those in his care. The woman is a custodian of her husband's house and is responsible for those in her care." [Bukhari]

Commentary: Whatever titles we have attached to our selves, those titles are not for showing off and boasting. Rather, each title comes with many responsibilities. Every person will be questioned regarding their responsibility, according to the scope of the responsibility they have been given in the position they have taken up. Hence, every husband and every wife needs to fulfill the responsibilities which come with the title of a husband or a wife. The fact that they both will be questioned regarding their position and responsibility should engender a sense of accountability and responsibility within them.

15. Prophet Muhammed ﷺ said, "The worst person is the one who is a harasser of his family." They asked, "O Messenger

of God! What is the sign that a person is a harasser of his family?" He said, "When the man enters the house, his wife becomes scared, and his child and his house worker scurry away. But when he leaves the house, his wife laughs and his family feel at ease." [Tabarani]

Commentary: The Prophet Muhammed ﷺ was a strong advocate as well as a wonderful model of a supportive and loving family man. He encouraged the men of his community to comfort and protect their families, to be gentle with their wives and children while at the same time making them feel secure and safe. Marriage offers tranquility to the soul and peace to the mind, so that the spouses may live together in an atmosphere of love, mercy, harmony, co-operation, mutual advice and tolerance, and lay the foundation for raising a healthy family in a nurturing, sound environment. Many men may feel that being rough, demanding, strict, or harsh is a sign of strength, but in fact, these qualities accomplish nothing but the deterioration of the family, striking fear and resentment in the hearts of wife and children and causing them to feel dread upon the man's arrival home. The Prophet Muhammed ﷺ realized that respect is earned through strength fashioned by love, tenderness, understanding, the sharing of wisdom, and the quiet fortitude of supporting and comforting the members of the family. Both men and women should find solace in their homes, should look forward to being together as a family unit, and feel that home is the one place in the world where they can find comfort and can be completely themselves, forgetting the pressures and demands of the outside world.

16. Prophet Muhammed ﷺ said, "The one who turns a wife against her husband is not from amongst us." [Abu Dawood]

Commentary: Unfortunately, there are people among us who revel in being a cause of dissension and disunity and who sow conflict and animosity between husbands and wives. There are people who make a living off trying their utmost to pit couples against each other until they resort to divorce. Gossip columns, tabloids, and even on a very local level, those people in our communities who spread rumors or encourage women or men to divulge the privacies of their marital life and who promote dissention between them all cause the breakdown of society. While of course, we should never encourage or ignore abuse between spouses, we should encourage married couples to have patience with one another, courage through hardship, and understanding through adversity. The Prophet Muhammed ﷺ understood that marriages could be compromised by petty issues and by the interference of outsiders with ill intentions. Hence, he made it a point to dissuade his community members from turning spouses from each other and getting involved with wrong intentions in the marital affairs of others.

17. Prophet Muhammed ﷺ said, "O God! I consider it a wrong action that the rights of two weak ones be violated: orphans and women." [Nasaee]

Commentary: The orphans and the women have almost universally been mistreated throughout human history, as they both have vulnerabilities that have left them open to societal bullying. They are usually not given their inheritance rights and are deprived from that which is rightfully theirs. So the teachings of Prophet Muhammed ﷺ advise us that it is morally as well as religiously wrong to deprive orphans and the women their due rights. Misogynistic statements and sexist jokes that degrade women need to be eradicated from our conversations. We sadly live in a time where violence against women and misogyny continue to thrive. Prophet Muhammed ﷺ through his actions and words persistently reminded men to respect women. If a society or certain cultures is going against these teachings, then it is the culture which needs to be condemned and not the religion which they claim to adhere to. Religion does not teach people to disrespect orphans and women. So it is not because of religion that people mistreat others. It is because of the lack of true understanding of the religion that people behave in a deplorable way. The teachings of Islam guide us to be respectful towards all human beings and specifically towards those in our communities who may be more vulnerable to abuse and neglect.

Respect for Relatives

18. Abu Hurayrah (R.A.) said, "A man came to Prophet Muhammed ﷺ and said, 'Messenger of God! I have relatives with whom I try to join ties of relationship but they sever relations with me. I treat them kindly but they reciprocate that by treating me badly. They behave foolishly towards me while I am forbearing towards them.' The Prophet said, 'If things are as you said, it is as if you were putting hot ashes in their mouths and a helper will perpetually be with you from God as long as you continue to do that.'" [Muslim]

Commentary: We are advised to be kind and respectful towards our relatives even if they behave disrespectfully with us. "Putting hot ashes in their mouths" is a metaphor for the pain of guilt that these types of people will feel because of your kind treatment towards them. They will feel ashamed of themselves because of how kindly they are being treated regardless of their own failure to reciprocate.

Upholding the ties of kinship is one of the core teachings of the Islamic faith. It is not just a matter of spending money or giving gifts—it goes much further than that. These ties are upheld by caring for poorer relatives, by visiting our family members to reinforce our relationships, by spreading love and kindness, by advising and helping one another selflessly, by speaking kindly to our relatives and asking about their wellbeing, by greeting them warmly with a smiling face and a caring attitude, and any other deed which will fill hearts with love and extend ties of mutual support among one's relatives. The pinnacle of good character is being respectful with those who mistreat us.

We have already seen how Islam encourages us to treat our parents with kindness and respect, even if they are non-Muslim, and now we see how it encourages us to treat our relatives equally well, regardless of their background, religious beliefs, or even their treatment of us.

19. Prophet Muhammed ﷺ said, "A young person never takes care of an old person due to age but that God facilitates someone to take care of the person when the person reaches that age." [Tirmidhi]

Commentary: We can refer to this as the boomerang principle—in other words, Prophet Muhammed ﷺ is trying to get across, 1,400 years ago, "what goes around comes around" or similarly, the Eastern spiritual idea of karma. When we make it a point to generate positive output, we can hope for positive input. When our parents and our relatives become old, we should be taking care of them just like how they went out of their way to take care of us when we were children. This is the basic idea of the circle of life. As human beings, we should not abandon our parents and relatives specifically and people in general in their old age; we must maintain every religion's promotion of the dignity and welfare of the elderly, the upholding of their honor for the wisdom of experience they possess and for the contributions they have made to our lives and to our communities.

Respecting Neighbors

20. Mujahid reported that a sheep was slaughtered for Abdullah ibn Amr (R.A.). He asked his servant, "Have you given any to our Jewish neighbor? I heard the Messenger of God ﷺ say, "Angel Gabriel kept on recommending that I treat my neighbors well until I thought that he would order me to treat them as my inheritors." [Bukhari]

Commentary: A strong emphasis has been placed through the teachings of the Prophet of Mercy to be kind towards neighbors irrespective of the religion of the neighbor. In our modern Western society, and even throughout the world, we as a human race are becoming more and more isolationist. With the dawn of the "modern era," the Internet, and so many other technological advances that allow us to "keep in touch" without the necessity of face-to-face contact, we are beginning to lose sight of the importance of personal relationships and friendliness to those surrounding us. With all this technology and with our fast-paced world, we may not even know what our neighbors looks like, let alone know them on a more personal level. Do we know the names of our neighbors? Have we been kind to them? Did we welcome them when they moved in? Do we treat our neighbors based on their color or race or language or do we treat them kindly just because they are our neighbors? By remembering back to a slower, more personal time when people not only knew their neighbors, but befriended them, shared meals with them, and looked after them, we can rekindle the spirit of neighborliness that the Prophet encouraged.

This emphasis on neighborliness was not simply meant to be an exercise in kindness, although surely, it was an effort to build the personal character of his followers. The Prophet's insistence on showing care and concern for neighbors, without regard for their background, religion, ties of kinship, etc. was also an effort of his part to show his followers how to build a strong community. A true and lasting community cannot be divided on superficial lines, but must be guarded and solidified through the development of strong personal relationships. We don't allow our children to play outside on the street as much anymore because we aren't secure enough to trust those in our neighborhood to watch out for everyone like they watch out for their own. The Prophet wanted to build a community where the children could play and parents could trust that they would be safe and looked after by all the adults. The Prophet wanted to build a community where the ill and elderly were known, respected and cared for. The Prophet wanted to build a community fortified by trust, by friendship, by loyalty and by dignified honor. His emphasis on neighborliness was not just to perfect the character of his followers, but also to show them how a functional society should be built.

21. Prophet Muhammed ﷺ said, "A true believer is not the one whose hunger is satiated while his neighbor remains hungry." [Bukhari in AM=Bukhari in Al-Adabul Mufrad]

Commentary: The Prophet of Mercy reminds us that we should not forget those who have less than us. If our neighbor does not have enough to eat, we should share our food with them as much as possible. If there are no needy neighbors, then we should not forget the hungry living in our towns and cities. We cannot ignore our neighbor's poverty and difficulty while we live a life of ease and plenty.

This is a truly interesting social concept, as it does make each and every one of us our brother's keeper. It also flies in the face of the individualistic "pull yourself up by your bootstraps" mentality that many have tried to espouse. The model that the Prophet taught is much more community-based, emphasizing the health of the community as a dependent variable based on the health of each individual. And throughout history, the societies that have flourished the longest were those that ensured the safety, security and basic welfare of its citizens. We are now just beginning to see the disastrous effects of laissez faire capitalism in the United States with huge gaps between the rich and the poor, staggering unemployment for the bottom 20% with simultaneous staggering wealth for the top 1%, increasing homelessness and mental illness, and unbearable debt borne by the shrinking middle class. These phenomena are not shocking—they are the spawn of selfishness, greed, and utter individualism. These social trends develop in a society that emphasizes the individual at the expense of the community. The Prophet knew that the stronger society would be one in which everyone was comfortable, rather than one in which some were living in heavenly luxury while others starved. The former society is more sustainable, less susceptible to internal strife and resentment, more balanced and morally sound.

22. Prophet Muhammed ﷺ was asked, "Messenger of God! A certain woman prays in the night, fasts in the day, does pious actions and gives charity, but injures her neighbors with her tongue." The Messenger of God said, "There is no good in her. She is one of the people of the Fire." They said, "Another woman prays the prescribed prayers and gives bits of curd (cheese like food) as charity and does not injure anyone." The Messenger of God said, "She is one of the people of Paradise." [Bukhari in AM]

Commentary: The Prophet of Mercy advises us that it is not enough that a person merely takes care of their own religious rituals, but rather, part of faith also entails that we do not physically or emotionally hurt our neighbors. Being an evil neighbor will eat away our pious noble deeds and actions. We should not do things to intentionally make our neighbors feel bad.

On a broader scale, the Prophet was announcing through this hadith that religious prescribed and recommended deeds (in Arabic called *Ibadah*) cannot be enough to save one's soul if they do not result in the practitioner's good behavior toward others. The purpose of worship is not only to bring the practitioner closer to God, but also to help perfect the character of the practitioner so that he or she can be a productive and beneficial member of society. Therefore, the Islamic faith tells us that our acts of worship are not enough to gain us the favor of God, we must supplement our acts of worship with the avoidance of evil deeds and the practice of beneficial ones.

23. Prophet Muhammed ﷺ said, "Muslim women! Muslim women! A woman should not belittle her female neighbor's gift, even if it is only a sheep's foot (hoof)." [Bukhari]

Commentary: The Prophet of Mercy advises us that we should value every gift of our neighbor or anyone else in general. We should not feel that since we gave them an expensive gift, why are they giving us a cheap gift? It's the thought that counts as is often said. We shouldn't look at a gift with a "what was the person thinking" look.

This hadith can obviously be applied to everyone, irrespective of gender, but it was specifically addressed to the women of the community because women tend to gossip and judge more than men. Therefore, this hadith was warning the women of the community to be grateful and gracious and to avoid being overly-critical and reaping bad deeds through gossip.

24. Anas (R.A.) reported that a Jewish boy used to serve Prophet Muhammed ﷺ. The boy became ill and the Prophet went to visit him. He sat by his head and said, "Become a Muslim." The boy looked at his father who was also sitting by his head. His father said to him, "Obey Abul-Qasim (a nickname of Prophet Muhammed ﷺ)." So the boy became a Muslim. The Prophet left saying, "Praise be to God who has saved him from the Fire!" [Bukhari]

Commentary: The Prophet of Mercy did not have any innate hatred towards Jewish people. As can been seen from the above, a Jewish boy was working for him and when the boy fell ill, the Prophet went to visit him. As is the desire of every prophet, the Prophet of Mercy wanted the boy to enter into the folds of Islam and accept the message he had received from God. The father gave consent to the boy and he eventually entered into Islam out of his own choice. History bares testimony to this fact that there is not even one incident from

Prophet Muhammed ﷺ's life which shows that he forced someone to convert to Islam. Even though his neighbors were cruel to him, he always reciprocated that cruelty with kindness.

The beauty of this story also lies in the boy's reaction to the Prophet's request that he convert to Islam. The boy looks to his father. Perhaps the boy was looking for approval, perhaps for support, perhaps for encouragement. Regardless, there is an emphasis through this hadith on the respect and due process those who wish to convert to Islam should maintain for their parents. While parents should not prevent their children from choosing Islam, the parents of those who wish to convert should be honored and given the respect of their parental station in life. Of course, there are conditions that may warrant different actions, but in general, parents should be given the respect of being introduced to the idea of conversion, of being given the reasons for the choice and of being loved and honored throughout the process. This boy displayed his respect for his father by simply looking at him in a way that the father understood was full of admiration, respect, and dignity.

Animal Rights

25. Prophet Muhammed ﷺ said, "A woman punished her cat by imprisoning it until it died of hunger and because of it, she will enter the Fire. It will be said to her, "You did not feed it or give it water when you imprisoned it nor did you release it and let it eat from the vermin and plants of the earth." [Bukhari]

Commentary: The Prophet of Mercy and his teachings of Islam were not only a source of mercy to human beings, but were also a source of mercy to every single thing on this earth. In this beautiful narration, we see how the woman will be deprived from entry into Paradise because of her cruelty to a helpless animal. Recently, a British bank worker was videotaped throwing a cat into a trash can. The video of that attack went viral, justifiably sparking outrage worldwide. These types of people, who obviously do not feel compassion or empathy for those that are helpless and dependent, are also those, in Islam's teachings who will not receive the compassion or empathy from God when they meet God in a helpless and dependent state.

26. Prophet Muhammed ﷺ said, "A prostitute was forgiven by God, because, passing by a panting dog near a well and seeing that the dog was about to die of thirst, she took off her shoe, and tying it with her head-cover she drew out some water for the dog. So, God forgave her because of that." [Bukhari]

Commentary: Once again we see how important it is for us to be kind and considerate to animals. Treating animals in a nice manner is held as an act worthy of praise. Islam's concern for animals goes beyond the prevention of physical cruelty; it enjoins on people to take responsibility of all creatures in the spirit of a positive philosophy of life and to be their active protectors. There is a larger concept at work here besides simply kindness toward animals. The global philosophy behind these Islamic teachings is that those in a position of power or dominance should take care and have moral responsibility over those in their domain—whether they are other people, plants, or animals. The spirit of this hadith can be seen woven through many other Islamic teachings regarding those in power—from kings to heads of households to religious leaders. The teaching is consistent throughout—those with the upper hand must deal justly and without cruelty or abuse toward those over whom they preside.

27. Prophet Muhammed ﷺ said, "Do not treat the backs of your beasts as pulpits." [Abu Dawood]

Commentary: The following statement of the Prophet of Mercy should be enough to stand on its own as a commentary: "Fear God regarding these mute animals (horses, camels, donkeys, etc.); mount them when they are sufficiently rested and dismount from them before tiring them." [Abu Dawood]

28. Abdullah (R.A.) reported that Prophet Muhammed ﷺ stopped in a place and then someone took a bird's eggs and the bird began to beat its wings around the head of the Messenger of God. He asked, "Which of you has taken its eggs?" A man said, "Messenger of Allah, I have taken its eggs." The Messenger of God said, "Return them out of mercy to the bird." [Bukhari in AM]

Commentary: The Prophet of Mercy is showing his compassion once again by requesting his companion to return the eggs to the distressed bird. Such amazing benevolence being shown to birds should help us realize how kind he was towards those around him, humans and animals. Abstention from physical cruelty to animals is not enough—refraining from mental cruelty is equally important. In the above incident, a bird's emotional distress has been treated as seriously as a physical injury and hence Islam promotes the idea that all creatures should live in peace if possible and that we as humans, even though we have been given domain over the animals of this world, should not wreak havoc in the land by harming animals, either physically or emotionally.

29. Prophet Muhammed ﷺ said, "Once, while a prophet amongst the prophets was taking a rest underneath a tree, an ant bit him. The prophet, therefore, ordered that his luggage be taken away from underneath that tree and then ordered that the dwelling place of the ants should be set on fire. God sent him a revelation, "Wouldn't a single ant (that bit you) have been sufficient?" [Bukhari]

Commentary: A prophet of the past is being rebuked by God for taking out his anger on the dwelling place of the ants and engaging in what we today call "collective punishment." If he wanted to exact revenge, then one ant was sufficient for him to be angry at. But there was no need to set the whole colony of ants on fire. We should also remember that we should not be hurting and killing insects and ants and similar creatures if they are not of any harm to us. The revelation of Islam came to civilize mankind and to help put limits on man's actions in every regard—even down to how we treat creatures as small and seemingly insignificant as ants. This Hadith is not just one dealing with the treatment of animals, but more generally speaking, it warns us against taking out our anger or judging entire groups by the actions of one or few of its members.

30. Prophet Muhammed ﷺ said, "God will ask on the Day of Judgment those who unjustly kill a sparrow." [Muslim]

Commentary: PETA (People for the Ethical Treatment of Animals), please add the above statement of Prophet Muhammed ﷺ on your website! As mentioned in the above narration, we should not kill any animate being just for the sake of hunting. We should not go around killing animals just for the sake of target practice. Blood sport was declared unlawful 1,400 years ago by the great Prophet Muhammed ﷺ: "The Prophet condemned those who use a living creature as a target." [Bukhari] Ibn 'Umar happened to pass by a party of men who had tied a hen and were shooting arrows at it. When they saw Ibn 'Umar coming, they scampered off. Ibn 'Umar angrily remarked, "Who has done this? Verily! God's Messenger has invoked a curse upon one who does this kind of thing." [Muslim]

The idea of this Hadith again is one of justice. Justice is the cornerstone of so many Islamic teachings. Our actions must be guided by this principle, this value. Hence, when we consider the treatment of animals, whether it is their treatment on an individual level as our pets, or on a collective level as pests or as prey, we must weigh with a just moral compass, the effects of our actions. And this lesson is not just one reserved for the treatment of animals. These Islamic teachings are ones that apply specifically but they also apply universally. These Hadith are attempts by the Prophet to teach global ideas of justice using easy-to-understand extended metaphors. Sparrows should not be killed unjustly...neither should civilians during wartime...neither should a village's crops, etc. This hadith gets us to think—yes, about our treatment of animals and helpless creatures, but also about how we act toward everyone and everything we encounter in any circumstance and ensure that it is with justice and fairness that we conduct ourselves.

Taking Care of the Environment

31. Prophet Muhammed ﷺ said, "If any believer plants any plant and a human being or an animal eats from it, he will be rewarded as if he had given that much in charity." [Muslim]

Commentary: Part of taking care of the environment is to make sure that there are enough trees in the world to maintain equilibrium in the ecosystem. The incentive for planting trees is that whoever benefits from the tree, be they a human or an animal, that act will be regarded as the noble act of charity. Charity is not only limited to donating money. Charity also extends to noble acts like planting trees, helping the poor and the indigent, meeting someone with a smiling face, and similar noble actions. This hadith also encourages the cultivation of productive crops. When a person is able, he should try to cultivate productive plants that can be used to feed others—this promotes local business, charity, sustainability, organic and healthy eating, and universal health. The use of others of such a plant is not only an act of charity toward the individual, but for the community as a whole.

32. Prophet Muhammed ﷺ said, 'If the Day of Judgment is about to take place while any one of you has a sapling in his hand which he can cultivate before the Day of Judgment takes place, let him cultivate it, for he will be rewarded for it." [Ahmad]

Commentary: We see how important the act of planting a tree is that even if the world is about to come an end and a person has the time to plant a tree, the person should do so. This hadith also begs the questions of us—What part have we played in preserving the greenery of Earth? Are we adding to the degradation of Earth or are we striving to protect it so that the future generations can benefit from it as well? How "green" are we in our day to day activities? How detrimental is our carbon footprint on a daily basis? Have we switched from using plastic shopping bags to degradable bags? Are we harming the environment for the sake of a little bit of extra profit to please our shareholders? We all must contribute our share in improving the environment for the sake of our beautiful planet Earth, God's gift to us.

33. Prophet Muhammed ﷺ said, "If anyone brings to life a dead land, he will have the reward for it, and what any creature eats of it will count as charity from him." [Nasai]

Commentary: The Prophet of Mercy is advising us to be merciful and kind to even the piece of land which is dead and which cannot grow anything from it. Since dead land is going to waste and it may be able to be used to grow crops to feed the community, especially it's impoverished, we are advised to make an effort to irrigate it and cultivate it and if we do, it is considered as a form of charity. Do we see potential in land that may seem barren and dry? Perhaps we can use creative means to cultivate land, no matter how big or small a plot, and no matter how dry and desolate. There are now hanging and urban gardens, drip lines and other creative means to cultivating areas that seemed useless before.

34. Prophet Muhammed ﷺ said, "Beware of the three acts that cause others to curse you: relieving yourselves in a watering place, on foot paths or shaded places." [Abu Dawood]

Commentary: The Prophet of Mercy once again reminds us that we need to take care of the environment around us and make every attempt to distance ourselves from irritating others with how we use the land. Hence, as mentioned in the above, urinating in places which are used by people should be avoided because it elicits curses from people who use those places. Similarly, let us use the resources of Earth today in such a way that we do not abuse it. Otherwise, people will one day curse us for polluting this beautiful planet. Let us do more to protect the environment and the water and the air amongst other things. Let us strive to leave behind a world better than how we found it for the children who will be born in the future.

Importance of Knowledge

35. Prophet Muhammed ﷺ said, "A believer never stops seeking knowledge until the believer enters paradise." [Tirmidhi]

Commentary: The first verse of the Noble Quran revealed to Prophet Muhammed ﷺ was: "Read in the name of your Lord who has created (all that exists)!" [Quran: Chapter 96, Verse 1]. The combination of this initial revelation and the above hadith illustrates the emphasis Islam puts on the search for knowledge. Islam is not a religion or a way of life that demands or even desires blind faith from its followers. Islam urges, encourages, and in fact demands and even dares its followers to go out and seek knowledge, question the tenets of the faith, learn from the scholars and obtain opinions from a variety of sources. Allah is perfectly confident in the truth of Islam and hence wants His followers to soak up as much knowledge and information from every available source because He knows that the more knowledge a person obtains, the more he will appreciate and see the wisdom of Islam.

Again and again, Islam iterates the importance of education and scholarship. The Prophet understood that, although he himself was unlettered, in order to be preserved, the religion and teachings would have to be maintained by the scholars and would have to be explained by people of knowledge. He also desired to promote a society and civilization that excelled in all facets of life, from politics to economics, science to architecture, art to the humanities. Just as Islam is a complete way of life, so too do its followers need to seek knowledge from all arenas in order to create a society based on Islamic teachings. Knowledge is wealth and we all need to immerse ourselves in it.

36. Prophet Muhammed ﷺ said, "The seeking of knowledge is obligatory for every believer." [Tirmidhi]

Commentary: The Prophet of Mercy reminds us that seeking knowledge is so important that God made the acquisition of knowledge mandatory for every follower of Islam—men and women alike. In our modern world, the people of many so-called "Muslim" countries such as Afghanistan are taking measures to prevent the seeking of knowledge, particularly by women. Girls and women who have sought knowledge have been attacked, even killed, for their efforts to follow the mandates of their religion to seek knowledge. Those in power who skew the teachings of Islam for their own benefit try to keep true understanding away from the citizenry because they know that knowledge is power, knowledge is enlightening, knowledge frees entire populations from the bounds of tyrants. Religion should not be blamed if people do not provide adequate opportunities for women to increase their knowledge.

Spending in Charity/Helping the Poor

37. Prophet Muhammed ﷺ said, "Every believer has to spend in charity." The companions said, "O Prophet of God! What if a person has nothing to give?" He said, "The person should work with their hands and benefit himself and also give in charity." They said, "If the person is unable to do that?" He said, "The person should help the needy who appeal for help." They said, "If the person cannot do that?" He said, "The person should perform all that is good and keep away from all that is evil and this will be regarded as charity." [Bukhari]

Commentary: The beautiful all-encompassing statement from the Prophet of Mercy reminds us that even if a person is poor and has no money, he must work with his hands and sacrifice to give charity. However, while this may seem stringent, the Muslims are also told that the charity that they give is actually a reward for them, so every act of charity is also a benefit to the giver, not only to the receiver. The inspiring statement goes on to mention that if anyone cannot do that then the person must help a person who is in distress. If that too is beyond the capability of the person, then the person must invite others towards piety and if the person is unable to that too then the person must make sure that at least he or she does not hurt anyone. All these things come under the umbrella of charity. The most remarkable aspect of this hadith is also a global concept in Islam—the teachings of Islam try to make a way for the believer, no matter his circumstance, to please his Lord. Islam never purports to be a way of life that makes the believer extend himself beyond his means. This hadith is an example—letting the believers know that, no matter their financial situation, they can still be a charitable giver.

38. Prophet Muhammed ﷺ said, "God will say, 'I asked you for food and you did not feed Me.' He will say, 'Lord, how could I feed You when You did not ask me for food and You are the Lord of the universe?' God will say, 'Did you not know that My slave so-and-so asked you for food and you did not feed him? Did you not know that if you had fed him, you would have found (the reward of) that action with Me? Son of Adam, I asked you for water and you did not give Me water.' The servant will reply, 'O Lord, how could I give you water when You are the Lord of the universe?' God will say, 'My servant so-and-so asked you for water and you did not give him water. Did you not know that if you had given him water, you would have found (the reward of) that action with Me? Son of Adam, I was ill and you did not visit Me.' He will say, 'O Lord, how could I visit You when You are the Lord of the universe?' God will say, 'Did you not know that My servant so-and-so was ill? If you had visited him you would have found (the reward of) that action with Me.'" [Bukhari in AM]

Commentary: The above interesting statement should inspire us to feed the hungry, quench the thirst of the thirsty, visit the sick and carry out other philanthropic acts. The teachings of Prophet Muhammed ﷺ place great importance on social life, civic engagement, and helping out the needy members of our society. Similar inspiring teachings as the above statement is also found in the Bible, such as in the book of Matthew, chapter 25, verse 35. This hadith also reminds us that our actions are like pebbles thrown into a clear pond—they may be small stones, but once they hit the water, their ripples reverberate and have much greater implications. Some have even mentioned that the flap of a butterfly's wings affects the wind patterns around the globe. Similarly, our actions may not seem like they will have earth-shattering implications, but in fact, each of our actions, each of our words, are acts that not only have immediate effect, but also affect our relationship with our Lord and our eternal position.

39. Prophet Muhammedﷺ said, "When a man spends on his family and sincerely hopes to be rewarded for it, it is a form of charity for him." [Bukhari]

Commentary: The Prophet of Mercy encourages us to spend on our family members by informing us that we should never feel that whatever we spend on our family members will go to waste. Spending on our family members is a form of charity as well when it is bolstered by sincere intentions. Whatever we spend on them for, be it be food, or clothing, or their education, or anything else beneficial, it is all meritorious and a person will be rewarded for it. Today, economists are trying to deter parents from having children by scaring them by saying that it will cost nearly $200,000 to raise one child till the age of 18. Even if we accept this figure to be correct, we spend on them with the intention that we will be rewarded for it.

Parents complain in their old age that there is no one there to look after them but the fault also lies with the parents (as well as with the kids for being selfish and neglectful) because of intentionally having only one or two children. It becomes a burden on the single child to take care of his parents in their old age so he usually abandons them. If parents had three to four children at least, it would become easier for them all to take care of their parents by sharing the responsibility of taking care of the aging parents. Hence, the charity that we give to our family to help raise it will come back to us not only after our death, but also during our lives in the form of lasting, good relationships and help in our older years.

Good Character

40. Prophet Muhammed ﷺ said, "The most beloved of God's servants to God are those with the best manners." [Tabarani]

Commentary: Manners are emphasized in Islam again and again. This is because our manners affect each and every one of our actions and therefore have far-reaching consequences. Islam guides our manners and hence guides our lives. Character development is the most important aspect of Islam because communities, societies, and the global order are all dependent on the character of the individuals who comprise them. The Prophet of Mercy reminds us to deal with others in the best of manners. Never be rude, or harsh, or mean to others. Everything considered to be bad manners should be abstained from. We need to be cognizant that when we interact with others in a good manner, people will hopefully reciprocate that kind gesture and treat us with respect as well.

41. Prophet Muhammed ﷺ said, "Shall I not inform you about the best of characters of the dwellers of this world and that of the hereafter? It is: maintain relationship with the person who cuts it off from you, give to the one who deprives you, and pardon the one who oppresses you." [Bayhaqi]

Commentary: The Prophet of Mercy explains brilliantly that we should treat others with good manners even if they do not return kindnesses. Even if the other person is trying to cut off relationships with us or is trying their utmost to deprive us of some benefit or is oppressing us, we should not reciprocate that with bad behavior. Our nice way of dealing with them will hopefully make them realize that their rudeness and their animosity is pointless. The Law of

Reciprocity teaches us that if we are nice to others, others will be nice to us. If we are mean to others, others will be mean to us. The Law of Reciprocity can really motivate us to be kind and nice to everyone around us and can be a catalyst to build a caring and compassionate community. And even if reciprocation is not received, the development of good character is a gift and benefit in itself and rewards the practitioner with God's grace even if he is not shown respect in this life.

42. Prophet Muhammed ﷺ said, "Love for humanity what you love for yourself." [Bukhari]

Commentary: The above is the Islamic version of the Golden Rule. The same rule is found in various religious scriptures:

— *Brahmanism:* This is the sum of duty: Do naught unto others which would cause you pain if done to you. [Mahabharata 5:1517]

— *Buddhism:* Hurt not others in ways that you yourself would find hurtful. [Udana Varga 5:18]

— *Confucianism:* Surely it is the maxim of loving-kindness: Do not unto others that you would not have them do unto you. [Analects 15:23]

— *Taoism:* Regard your neighbor's gain as your own gain, and your neighbor's loss as your own loss. [T'ai Shag Kan Ying P'ien]

— *Zoroastrianism:* That nature alone is good which refrains from doing unto another whatsoever is not good for itself. [Dadistan-i-dinik 94:5]

— *Judaism:* What is hateful to you, do not to your fellowmen. That is the entire Law; all the rest is commentary. [Talmud, Shabbat 31a]

— *Christianity:* In everything, therefore, treat people the same way you want them to treat you. [Matthew 7:12]

[Source: Wikipedia]

43. Prophet Muhammed ﷺ said, "Beware of jealousy, for verily it destroys good deeds the way fire destroys wood." [Abu Dawood]

Commentary: They say that a jealous person dies a thousand deaths. A jealous person will be deprived from a life of happiness because the person will never be happy with what he has and will constantly be looking at what others have which he does not have. The desires of the human being are limitless and hence they can never be fulfilled. We are jealous today because of someone's beauty, or house, or vehicle, or status, or wealth, or intellect and other materialistic things. We should realize, however, that there are many who have less than us so we should be happy with what we have and we should not desire that others are deprived from what they have. Also, jealousy will never satisfy any of our feelings—it will leave us feeling hollow and dissatisfied, angry and spiteful whereas, gratitude will fill us with joy and happiness, fullness and love.

44. Anas said, "I served Prophet Muhammed ﷺ for ten years. He never said 'uff' to me and he never said about anything I had not done, "Why didn't you do it?" or about something I had done, "Why did you do that?" [Muslim]

Commentary: What amazing character! No wonder people flocked to him and preferred to live with him over staying with their own parents. The Prophet not only had the highest quality of personal character, but also had stunning charisma. He led his community through kindness, service, and by his own example. This hadith serves to teach those who wish to lead how they can influence and inspire others through gentleness and grace rather than through harshness and brute power. It also goes to show that Islam came to perfect society so that all strata of the community, from leaders to those that served them could live in harmony if the perfection of character and manners was their guide. Such amazing human beings rule over people's hearts, not by brute force, but through magnificent character.

45. Prophet Muhammed ﷺ said, "True wealth does not mean having a lot of property. But rather, true wealth is in being content." [Bukhari]

Commentary: Wow! Such amazing advice which our consumer-based society can really benefit from! We are under this false impression that the more a person has, the more successful a person is; there is even a famous license plate frame that reads "The person who dies with the most toys wins." The Prophet of Mercy negates this false notion and beautifully explains to us that real wealth is obtained when our heart and mind are happy with whatever we have. While jealousy and envy of material things is like a poison to the soul, gratitude breeds contentment and tranquility. That is true wealth. If we keep this in mind, then we will find so much happiness in our lives and peace will permeate our earthly existence. Today, we are geared towards looking at what others have, which in turn keeps us away from being content with what we have. Yes, we should try our best to excel in every possible way, and attaining material wealth is not wrong, but it should not be an end in itself, but rather a means to bettering our world. But if we cannot get something, or we do not have something, that should not depress us. Be happy with what you have because that is true wealth!

46. Prophet Muhammed ﷺ said, "Whoever is offered an apology from a fellow believer should accept it unless he knows that the person apologizing is being dishonest." [Mishkat]

Commentary: The Prophet of Mercy reminds us that it is considered to be an act of good character when we accept the apology of a sincerely remorseful person. At times, because of our egos and because of our self-centeredness, we are very slow in accepting the apology of others even though others are apologizing to us repeatedly. In this day and age, when people rarely apologize, we should extend a hand of forgiveness by accepting the apology of the one who is sincere. Instead, we often remain cynical of apologies. We should look for excuses to accept people's apologies, as forgiveness is the key to progress and is the key that unlocks the door to harmonious relations and genteel society.

47. Prophet Muhammed ﷺ said, "Be kind, for whenever kindness becomes a part of something, it beautifies it. Whenever it is taken from something, it leaves it tarnished." [Bukhari in AM]

Commentary: The beautiful statement informs us that we need to be kind to everything around us from the animals, to the environment and to people. As you have read the previous statements of Prophet Muhammed ﷺ and as you continue to read his statements in the upcoming pages, you will notice how kind and gentle Prophet Muhammed ﷺ was with every creation. When we are kind with others, it adds to our beauty and we become beloved because of our kind gentle disposition. Kindness makes us beautiful. Those who are harsh and rough in their dealings with others and are devoid of kindness may be feared but are never respected and their name remains tarnished in the minds of people. We affectionately remember throughout our lives those teachers who were kind in their dealings with us. We remember those superiors fondly who were gentle with us. We can't stand those mangers who are harsh and unkind with us. The absence of kindness from our lives today has wreaked havoc on our relationships with our parents, spouses, children, and co-workers. Acting upon these beautiful teachings of Prophet Muhammed ﷺ will engender within us kindness, generosity, mercy, sympathy, peace, truthfulness and many other noble characteristics towards every creation in all situations.

48. Prophet Muhammed ﷺ was asked, "How many times should we forgive the servant?" He replied, "Seventy times a day." [Tirmidhi] (The number seventy is used in the Arabic language to indicate something which is numerous.)

Commentary: The Prophet of Mercy reminds us that we are all prone to making mistakes not only on rare occasions but rather every single day of our life. Hence, when those people who we interact with on a daily basis make mistakes, we must treat them leniently. We should realize that no one makes a mistake intentionally. Our spouse, our child, or our co-worker will make mistakes, but we should be benevolent and forgive them. Of course steps should be taken so that the same mistake is not repeated. To err is human, to forgive, divine. This is similar to the Biblical teaching of Jesus when he warned against the stoning of the woman accused of adultery, saying to her chastisers, "Let he who has not sinned cast the first stone." [Book of John, Chapter 8] If we consider how many errors we make on a daily basis, how many times we commit sins, we will realize how much we need God's forgiveness. This realization should help us to be more forgiving of others since we will realize that we too are human and in need of forgiveness.

49. Prophet Muhammed ﷺ said, "The true believer is the one from whose tongue and hand other believers are safe." [Bukhari]

Commentary: If we want to be considered pious, then we must make sure that we do not hurt others with our tongues or with our hands. It is very easy to inflict mental pain and torture upon others with our tongues, but we should remember that just as we do not like other people to verbally abuse us, we should not abuse others as well. We should make sure that our spouses are safe from being abused by our tongues or our hands. We should not ridicule, lie, spread rumors, slander someone or falsely accuse anyone. At times, the pain inflicted by the tongue is worse than the pain inflicted by the hand and perhaps it is for that reason the Prophet Muhammed ﷺ mentioned the tongue before the hand in the above statement of his. In another hadith, the Prophet affirms the dangers of the tongue by stating that the majority of the people of hellfire will reach that destination because of words uttered by the tongue.

50. Prophet Muhammed ﷺ said, "A kind word is charity." [Bukhari]

Commentary: We should accustom ourselves to saying kind words, such as please, thank you, have a good day, sorry, and other similar phrases which exude kindness. They create love and affection and promote an environment of harmony and unity. The pristine concept of charity is not only limited to financial contributions—saying a kind word to others is also an act of charity because it brings happiness and joy to those on the receiving end.

51. Prophet Muhammed ﷺ said, "Should any of you burp or sneeze, let him stifle the sound." [Bayhaqi]

Commentary: It is considered rude when we burp or sneeze and we don't stifle ourselves. One simple way of acting upon this teaching is by covering our mouth with our palm when we burp to decrease the sound and to cover the mouth with the inside part of the elbow when we sneeze. It will also prevent the proliferation of germs. Again, Islam is not just about acts of worship, but also about the elevation of society through the perfection of character and manners. Islam promotes genteel, gracious, and upright social dealings and shuns rudeness, brutish and boorish manners.

52. Prophet Muhammed ﷺ said, "Anyone who does not show mercy to our children nor acknowledge the right of our old people is not one of us." [Bukhari in AM]

Commentary: The Prophet of Mercy exhorts us to be respectful to our elders and to be kind and compassionate towards youngsters. We should realize that our elderly have much more experience than us and the younger ones are more prone to mistakes and hence, they both deserve our utmost respect and benevolent behavior. When our parents and elders become old, we should not abandon them but rather look after them as they looked after us when we were growing up. It is their right of old age that others look after them. Islam promotes the concept of the circle of life, where each member of society is cared for and appreciated for their commitment to the community. Many in our modern world have abandoned this notion—some view children to be a burden instead of a blessing; child abuse, neglect, abandonment and exploitation have become daily phenomena. Similarly, the elderly have also been cast aside as burdensome; they are sent to retirement or convalescent homes to be visited on occasion or not at all, to be cared for by strangers and left to die. Their experience, wisdom and stories are not only unappreciated but often lost forever. This hadith warns that the believers of Islam must give these particularly vulnerable groups the respect, honor and good treatment they deserve.

53. The father of Abul Ahwas (R.A.) once asked Prophet Muhammed ﷺ, "If I pass by someone who does not offer me a place to rest or show me hospitality, and then he later comes my way, should I offer him hospitality or treat him as he treated me?" He ﷺ replied, "You should offer him hospitality." [Tirmidhi]

Commentary: What amazing teachings from the Prophet of Mercy! Just because someone is inhospitable to us and they are unkind and uncharitable towards us, it does not mean that we should behave in a similar manner. We need to move beyond treating others how they have mistreated us in the past, beyond the pettiness of tit for tat because we all know that this is an end game—there is no happy ending and this type of mistreatment leads only to a society filled with mistrust and coldness. Irrespective of if our relatives and friends have treated us cordially in the past or not, we should be cordial and treat them amiably and kindly. Eventually, this produces a society based on altruism and mutual care and concern. Other traditions and cultures have called it karma, paying it forward, or random acts of kindness. Regardless of the name we put to this type of behavior, the end result is a more open, charitable, warm community that cares for the needs of all its members.

Being Merciful

54. Prophet Muhammed ﷺ said, "A man came across a thorn on the road and said, 'I will remove this thorn so that it does not harm a believing person.' For that reason he was forgiven." [Bukhari in AM]

Commentary: While this hadith is about removing obstructions from the road to prevent injury to others, it has a much larger global meaning. The Prophet is trying to instill in the believers a constant sense of thoughtfulness and conscientiousness. The Prophet is teaching selflessness and the idea that we must always be thinking of how to protect and benefit our community. While the man himself saw the thorn in the road and simply could have avoided it himself, he went beyond himself and had compassion for his fellow human. Even though no one could reward him or appreciate his deed because it was a preventative one in nature, his selflessness and simple desire to ward off danger for others who might come across that same thorn gained him his reward with God. Islam came to promote this type of community—one in which its members, while themselves attempting to improve and be successful, are also concerned with the improvement and wellbeing of others.

55. Ibn Umar (R.A.) mentioned, "During some of the battles of God's apostle a woman was found killed, so God's apostle ﷺ forbade the killing of women and children." [Bukhari]

Commentary: The mercy to the world reminds us that our conduct during times of war must be honorable, and we should be merciful to the weak and unprotected, especially women and children. The

Prophet's companion, Abu Bakr, advised one of his military commanders with the following merciful proclamation, "Do not kill women or children or an aged, infirm person. Do not cut down fruit-bearing trees. Do not destroy an inhabited place." [Muwatta] While many in the media wish to paint Islam as a bellicose religion, in fact, the revelation of Islam and the teachings of the Prophet had the effect of civilizing conflict and restricting its reach through numerous limitations and rules of warfare. One of the rules included a provision in which non-combatants could not be intentionally harmed, including women and children, the weak and sick, the elderly, and those things that bring livelihood to a place, including its crops, buildings and infrastructure. Like so many other misconceptions floated about the religion of Islam, the concept of warfare in Islam has been misconstrued. In fact, warfare techniques of many countries are very barbaric, with the concept of civilian casualties and the destruction of homes and infrastructure relegated so simply to "collateral damage" or a "necessary evil."

56. Prophet Muhammed ﷺ said, "Do not wish to meet an enemy." [Bukhari]

Commentary: The merciful one reminds his followers once again to be merciful and discourages them from choosing conflict. Peace must be given a chance and peace must be given preference over conflict and war. Peace treaties should be encouraged even if that means that we will be compromising. The warmongers around the world should be ashamed of themselves for spilling so much innocent blood in the world. Jimi Hendrix said, "When the power of love overcomes the love of power, the world will know peace." Let us all strive our utmost to become instruments of peace and not war. Prophet Muhammed ﷺ disliked fighting and war and hence he discouraged his followers from wishing to meet an enemy and provoking a fight.

57. Aisha (R.A.) said, "I was on a camel which was proving to be difficult to ride on and Prophet Muhammed ﷺ remarked,

"You must be compassionate. Whenever there is compassion in something, it adorns it, and when it is removed from something it disgraces it." [Bukhari in AM]

Commentary: Being merciful and peaceful is not limited to only human beings, but the Prophet of Mercy even advises us to be kind and compassionate towards animals. We all should be advocates of animal rights and the responsibility of taking care of animal rights should not be left only to animal rights groups like PETA. Our compassion will be like a warm cloak for those suffering the chill of winter or a cool breeze to those under the oppression of the hot summer sun. Those who develop the characteristic of compassion cannot help but to sincerely care for others. Again, just like so many hadiths, the development of character will lead to a society that bolsters itself with goodness and whose members care for one another.

58. Prophet Muhammed ﷺ kissed (his grandson) Hasan ibn Ali (R.A.) while al-Aqra ibn Habis at-Tamimi (R.A.) was sitting with him. Al-Aqra said, "I have ten children and I have never kissed any of them." The Messenger of God looked at him and said, "Whoever does not show mercy will not be shown mercy." [Bukhari]

Commentary: Islam came and completely transformed the Arabian Peninsula with such beautiful teachings which are replete with emphasis on being merciful to every single creation of God including being kind and showing our love towards children. Not only does the Prophet in this hadith encourage the showing of mercy, but the open display of kindness and affection from a grown man toward his grandson is also encouraged. Many men think it is a sign of weakness to display affection or gentleness, but in fact, the Prophet is teaching his followers that the outward display of love (within the confines of propriety) is a positive thing and a way of attaining the grace of God.

59. A Bedouin urinated in the mosque. The people moved towards him (to stop him) and Prophet Muhammed ﷺ said, "Leave him alone and pour a bucket of water onto his urine. You were sent to make things easy for people and not to make them difficult." [Bukhari]

Commentary: From the above tradition, we learn a number of things: We should be gentle when dealing with someone who is ignorant and teach him gently and kindly what he needs to know, without being harsh with him. Prophet Muhammed ﷺ was thinking of the likely consequences of the two options—stopping him or leaving him alone. If they tried to stop him, forcing a man to suppress his urination could do him harm, and if he was unable to stop but moved away because he was afraid of them, the impurity would be spread over a wider area of the mosque and on the man's body and clothing. Furthermore, since the man was most likely ignorant of the desire to keep the mosque pure for the prayers, rebuking him roughly without explanation would have simply angered the man and distanced him from Islam. The Prophet had the foresight to see that leaving the man alone until he had finished urinating was the lesser of two evils, especially since the man had already started urinating, and it was a problem that they would be able to do something about by cleaning it afterwards. [Commentary From: The Prophet's Methods for Correcting People's Mistakes] So he told his companions to leave the Bedouin alone and not to interrupt him. Hence, we need to be gentle and soft in our approach especially with people whom we do not know and who are not previously aware of the "rules" or concepts we would like them to understand.

60. Prophet Muhammed ﷺ said, "Allah did not make anything permitted more hated to Him than divorce." [Hakim]

Commentary: While divorce is discouraged in Islam, it is allowed in cases when there exists conditions in either the man or woman that cannot be rectified. In such cases, the couple and their relatives should not worsen the situation by saying improper things. The problems that the couples have should not become a reason for other wrongs such as gossiping, accusing, belittling, or abusing etc. Such acts will only increase the hatred of the couple and their families. The sad fact is that divorce tears families apart, can leave children with emotional scars, and hurt and damage the family structure as a whole. Divorce should be the last resort in our marital conflicts.

Being Cheerful

61. Prophet Muhammed ﷺ said, "Every act of kindness is charity. Part of kindness is that you meet your brother with a cheerful face and you pour some water from your bucket into his water vessel." [Bukhari in AM]

Commentary: The Prophet of Mercy reminds us that we must be kind at all times and the result of it is that it is a form of charity as well. When we greet others, we should have a cheerful face and we should have a smile on our faces. In old times, people would draw water out from wells and they still do that in some countries. In such places, it would be considered an act of kindness to help the person next to them by pouring water into their bucket as well. In a modern context, one way of being kind is that if we are at the grocery store waiting for checkout, and the person behind us has far less in their cart, we should let that person go ahead because it will take longer for us to clear the cashier. So let us be kind to each other irrespective of the variance in our religion, culture, language, nationality, race, gender, color or anything else we use as an excuse to sow seeds of disunity. A needy person's race, religion, gender, or color should not be an impediment for us in lending a helping hand.

62. Jarir (R.A.) said, "Since the time I became a Muslim, the Messenger of God, never saw me without smiling at me." [Bukhari in AM]

Commentary: The Prophet of Mercy leads by example and acts upon the advice that he gives to others by showing that whenever he would meet anybody, he would smile. Let us implement this in our life and we will see that even those who are making the most incendiary remarks in our faces will calm down when we talk to them with a cheerful demeanor.

63. Prophet Muhammed ﷺ said, "Do not belittle any act of kindness, even that of greeting your brother with a cheerful face." [Muslim]

Commentary: The Prophet of Mercy reminds us once again that we should try to be as kind as possible to others and we should never think that any act of kindness is too small or insignificant. Even meeting anyone happily should not be considered insignificant. Every day we interact with others, so this teaching of meeting with a smile is extremely important. That is why I have chosen a third saying on the same theme for added emphasis.

Being Just

64. A woman named Fusayla said that she heard her father say, "I asked, "Messenger of God! Is it part of partisanship and tribalism for a person to help his people in something which is unjust?" "Yes!" he replied." [Bukhari in AM]

Commentary: The Prophet of Mercy reminds us about the importance of being fair and just by informing us that if we aid and abet people, even our own family, in an unjust activity, then that is blameworthy and reprehensible. It is abhorrent when leaders of our countries force us to side with them in their unjust decisions and then make unhelpful statements such as, "Either you are with us or against us!" We should be on the side of truth and justice, irrespective of it concurring with the decisions of the leaders of our tribes and countries or not.

65. Prophet Muhammed ﷺ said, "The worst of guardians is a cruel ruler. Beware of becoming one of them." [Muslim]

Commentary: The Prophet of Mercy reminds us that if a person is a leader, he or she must be gentle and kind towards those over which he or she rules. It is a shame that most of the cruelest leaders of the world are ruling so-called "Muslim" countries. Titles of leadership positions are not for name and fame. Those titles are there to fulfill the responsibilities which are attached with those titles. Sadly, we have many leaders who attach grand titles to their names, but they are not fulfilling the demands of those titles. Prophet Muhammed ﷺ loved just rulers irrespective of the faith of the ruler. That is why he ordered his persecuted companions to migrate to current day Ethiopia from Makkah, Saudi Arabia, because there was a just Christian ruler there.

66. Prophet Muhammed ﷺ said, "It is not lawful for anyone to cut himself off from his believing brother for more than three nights so that when they meet, one of them turns his face away in avoidance and the other one turns his face away as well. The better of them is the one who initiates the greeting." [Bukhari in AM]

Commentary: The Prophet of Mercy reminds us all that we do not sever our ties with our acquaintances for longer than three days to such an extent that we avoid each other. We all have disagreements, but they should not become grudges. If we don't get along with someone, that's fine. But we should never behave towards each other as mentioned in the above statement. At a minimum, when our paths cross, we should greet the other person. When we carry hatred in our hearts towards others, then we are the ones who will be deprived of happiness because of the animosity being pent up within us.

67. Prophet Muhammed ﷺ said, "Rights will be given to those to whom they are owed to on the Day of Rising until even the hornless sheep will have retaliation against the horned sheep." [Muslim]

Commentary: The Prophet of Mercy reminds us that on the Day of Judgment, every created thing will be treated justly and fairly. To such an extent that if a horned sheep hit a hornless sheep in the world, then on that day of reckoning, the horns will be switched and justice will be meted out. If the oppressed animal will be able to exact such revenge on the Day of Judgment, then what about us human beings who unjustly and unfairly treat others to such an extent that we have clinical terms such as 'collateral damage'! Many of today's leaders and warmongers have on their hands the blood of thousands of innocent people!

68. Prophet Muhammed ﷺ said, "Help your brother whether he is the oppressor or the oppressed." A man said, "O Messenger of God! I can help him if he is oppressed, but how do I help him if he is the oppressor?" The Messenger of God said, "You should prevent him from committing wrong and if you do prevent him then that will be considered as helping him." [Bukhari]

Commentary: The Prophet of Mercy reminds us that we must try our utmost to stop the oppressor whichever way we can. Many countries and tribes and people have oppressed others for the weakest of reasons and have displaced, injured, and killed thousands of people. We should ask ourselves if we did anything practical to stop the oppressor from his unjust behavior or did we ignore it? Did we raise our voices against the oppressor or not? Did we try to counsel the tyrant or not?

Restraining Anger

69. **Prophet Muhammed ﷺ said, "Who do you reckon to be a wrestler and a strong person? The one who most often throws people down (in a fight)?" They replied, "The wrestler is the one whom men do not throw down." He said, "No! The real wrestler is the one who controls himself when he is angry." [Bukhari in AM]**

Commentary: The Prophet of Mercy advises us that we need to control ourselves in moments of anger and if we do, then that is true strength. Throughout history, anger has been the downfall of many men and the cause of many tragedies. It is simple to fly off the handle at the slightest of annoyances. It is easy to curse, yell, and throw a fit. Much harder is it to acknowledge these feelings of aggravation, suppress them and express oneself in a civilized manner. Much more difficult, yet much more rewarding both in this life and the next, is to restrain one's urges toward anger and angry outbursts and to transform this anger into constructive, positive interactions. The Prophet, in this hadith, compares this restrained, controlled person with a wrestler, to personify how one must literally wrestle with one's emotions and pin them down, patiently and persistently gaining complete control over and submission from these feelings.

70. **Prophet Muhammed ﷺ said, "Teach and make things easy and not difficult. When one of you is angry, he should be silent." [Bukhari in AM]**

Commentary: The Prophet of Mercy was aware that teaching often can lead to frustrations with students and that these frustrations could often result in regrettable outbursts. It is better to remain silent when we are angry because many students have been scarred for life because their teachers mocked them and ridiculed them in front of their classmates. However, the Prophet was aware of the fact that teachers not only teach the subject matter that they have an expertise in, but they also teach by the example of their personalities. Teachers mold students not only in science, math, and history, but also in character and morals. Teachers therefore must exemplify patience to teach their students patience, restraint to teach their students restraint, and uprightness to teach their students uprightness.

71. Prophet Muhammed ﷺ said, "Listen attentively! The best of humans are those who are slow to get angry and quick to forgive. Pay attention! The worst of humans are those who get angry quickly and are slow to forgive." [Tirmidhi]

Commentary: The Prophet of Mercy reminds us that we need to restrain our anger and if we do, then we are considered the best of humans. With respect to anger, people are of four types: 1) Slow to get angry and slow to forgive. One cancels out the other. 2) Quick to get angry and quick to forgive. One cancels out the other. 3) Quick to get angry and slow to forgive. These are the worst of people. I'm sure we must have come across such people amongst our superiors, colleagues, relatives, or even our spouses. 4) Slow to get angry and quick to forgive. This fourth type of group of people are very few but they are the best of humans. May we be surrounded by such people and may our spouses and relatives and colleagues be walking examples of those who get angry very slowly and when they do get angry, they quickly forgive. Amen.

72. A man said to Prophet Muhammed ﷺ, "Give me some advice." The Prophet said, "Do not get angry." The man repeated his request several times and each time the Prophet said, "Do not get angry." [Bukhari]

Commentary: The sound advice from Prophet Muhammed ﷺ which has been mentioned in the preceding lines all show how important it is for all of us to restrain our anger. We unnecessarily become angry with our parents, spouses, children, relatives, employees, coworkers, colleagues, neighbors and people in general. It is about time we calmed down and became gentle in our dealings with others. Do we become angry when things do not go our way? Do we get angry when something happens contrary to what we expected? When we get angry, do we lose control of ourselves and say or do things which we regret later? Once things have calmed down, do we feel bad about how we behaved when we were angry? If we answered 'yes' to any of the previous questions, then we need to start working on anger management. People who do not control their anger are generally disliked by the people around them.

Mutual Relationships

73. **Bara ibn Azib (R.A.) said, "The Messenger of God instructed us to do seven things: He instructed us to visit the sick, to join funeral processions, to bless people who sneeze, to help the weak, to help the wronged, to accept invitations, to return the greeting, and to fulfill our oaths." [Bukhari]**

Commentary: How many of these deeds do we regularly act upon and consider them to be of importance? Every single one of the seven is a means of creating unity and strengthening the bond of social cohesion. When we ignore them, it is at the detriment of society and when we implement them, it is for the advantage of society. Acting upon them will build a strong bond of care and affection for others and ignoring them will erode communal care and affection. Again, we see a hadith about the building of communities around the concept of etiquette and positive manners flowing from one to another. The Prophet was a strong advocate of manners and he emphasized that the development of character would sustain a community, just as the deterioration of etiquette and goodwill toward our neighbors would be the downfall of society.

74. **Prophet Muhammed ﷺ said, "Never express joy at your fellow man's afflictions, for God just might free him of them and afflict you." [Tabarani]**

Commentary: Irrespective of if a person believes in God or not, it is very wrong to be happy when people experience difficulty and hardship in their lives. Today it is others who are going through tough times, and tomorrow, it could very well be us who might go through even tougher times. Hence, when someone goes through any affliction, the correct thing to do is to be sympathetic towards them and assist them as much as possible so that their difficult circumstance is alleviated from them. If we help others today in their times of need, they will help us tomorrow when we need them.

75. Prophet Muhammed ﷺ said, "Do not be people without minds of your own, saying that if others treat you well you will treat them well and that if they do wrong you will do wrong. But (instead) accustom yourselves to do good if people do good and not to do wrong if they do evil." [Tirmidhi]

Commentary: The Prophet of Mercy reminds us that our criterion for the kind treatment of others is not how they have treated us. Rather our benchmark is good manners and noble character at all times in all situations irrespective if others have been kind to us or not in the past. The "golden rule" does not say "treat others the way they treat you," but rather "treat others the way you would like to be treated." Similarly, the Prophet champions this type of noble behavior rather than the "what have you done for me lately" attitude pervasive in much of our modern society. Though this is not easy to do, it is what we should accustom ourselves to doing.

76. Prophet Muhammed ﷺ said, "Beware of suspicion for it is the most deceitful of thoughts." [Bukhari]

Commentary: The Prophet of Mercy reminds us about the importance of making sure that we do not become suspicious of people without any valid reason. When we become suspicious of people, then we lose trust in them. We blame them for things which they did not do and we attribute words to them which they never uttered. If we have no credible evidence about something, then we should not judge people on mere suspicion. When we become suspicious of our spouses or children or co-workers and we make decisions because of suspicion, and many times, things turn out to be false, then we are forced to embarrassingly apologize because of the lack of plausible evidence. Also, suspicion is the basis for over-thinking, and over-thinking is often the root of much larger problems. The suspicious person is constantly trying to analyze behavior in negative ways, constantly trying to fit the actions and words of others into their grand scheme of what might be instead of focusing on what is. Suspicion for no reason destroys relationships and leads both the suspicious and the suspect toward emotional chaos, again, without cause. The Prophet often warned against mischief makers, and the suspicious people are at the nucleus of mischief making. Suspicion is deception and we need to avoid it as much as possible.

77. Prophet Muhammed ﷺ said, "Give gifts and you will love one another." [Bukharin in AM]

Commentary: The Prophet of Mercy reminds us that if we want to increase mutual love and affection and unity between spouses or children or relatives or others, one good way of doing that is by giving gifts. Just as the Prophet espoused good manners and strong character, so too did he encourage his followers to practice generosity, selflessness and thoughtfulness. There are myriad examples of the Prophet himself doing random acts of kindness or acting in very thoughtful ways. He was a model of nobility and knew that his community would flourish if each individual took time to think about others and act toward them out of love and affection. This teaching is the opposite of many modern phenomena of greed, selfishness and instant gratification. I am open to accepting gifts at anytime of the year.

78. Prophet Mohammad ﷺ said, "Do you know what backbiting is?" They said, "God and His Messenger know best." He then said, "It is to say something about your brother (who is not present) that he would dislike." Someone asked him, "But what if what I say is true?" The Messenger of God said, "If what you say about him is true, you are backbiting him, but if it is not true then you have slandered him." [Muslim]

Commentary: We have been advised to not spread the faults and mistakes of human beings because backbiting and gossiping sows the seeds of enmity and discord amongst people. The Prophet is also known to have mentioned that the majority of the people in hellfire will have been punished because of words they uttered during their lifetime. The tongue is known to be the most dangerous weapon we can use and the Prophet was constantly warning his followers to guard themselves against backbiting and slander.

79. The Prophet ﷺ stood beside some people, who were seated and said, "Would you like me to distinguish between the best of you and the worst of you?" They remained silent, so he asked the same question three times. A man then said, "Certainly, O Prophet of God! Distinguish for us the best of us and the worst of us." The Prophet said, "The best of you is the one on whom good hopes are placed and no evil is expected; and the worst of you is the one on whom good hopes are not placed and from whose evil people are in constant danger." [Tirmidhi]

Commentary: What inspiring words from the amazing teachings of Prophet Muhammed ﷺ! The best of us are those on whom people place their hopes and expectations that we will be kind and courteous with them and they will feel safe when they are around us. The worst of us are those on whom no good hope is placed, but rather, they are so mean that people are always scared that we might harm them or lie about them or be mean to them or injure them or any other evil. Let us all strive to be the best of humans.

80. Prophet Muhammed ﷺ said, "The best person is the one who benefits other people the most." [Kanzul Ummal]

Commentary: The Prophet of Mercy is advising every one of us, irrespective of our religion, race, color, creed, gender, or nationality that the best people are those who are the most helpful to others. So let us take stock of ourselves and ask how helpful we have been to others? When was the last time we helped a needy person? When was the last time we donated to aid orphans and widows? Am I too absorbed with my luxuries that I haven't found the time to help others in whichever way possible? It does not matter how much wealth we have, or what our gender is, or what our religion is, but none of us have an excuse to ignore helping out others.

81. **Prophet Muhammed ﷺ said, "I saw a man going about in Paradise who was there on account of cutting down a tree which had been a nuisance to the believers which was in the middle of the road." [Muslim]**

Commentary: The Prophet of Mercy reminds us about the importance of being a source of mercy and blessings for those around us. Whichever way we can, we should try to help others. Whatever is inconveniencing others, we should try our utmost to remove that obstacle. That could mean cutting down a tree if it is hindering others, or mowing the grass if it is too long, or shoveling the snow, or removing glass from the pathways, or through many other means. Littering the environment, throwing peels, disposing of garbage on the streets, in a public place, lake or sea etc. is strongly discouraged. We are taught to maintain cleanliness at all times. In fact we are rewarded to take a moment to pick up and dispose of any litter or harmful object we find in our surroundings or pathways. Many people take this for granted. If we are not yet upon the level of picking up litter thrown by others then at least we should not be the litterbugs.

82. **Prophet Muhammed ﷺ said, "A man follows the religion and a way of life of his close friend, so each of you should be very careful about whom he takes as a close friend." [Abu Dawood]**

Commentary: The Prophet of Mercy reminds us to choose our friends wisely because we become like those who we associate with. Good friends are those who have good morals and ethics which we should be aspiring to perfect ourselves in. As parents, it is our responsibility to make sure that our children have friends who are good role models for our children.

83. **Prophet Muhammed ﷺ said, "Wonderful is the case of a believer. There is good for him in everything, and it is for the believer alone. If he experiences a blessing, he is grateful and that is good for him. If he experiences an adversity he is patient and that is also good for him." [Muslim]**

Commentary: When we experience something good in our life then we should be thankful to the people around us and if we believe in a supreme being, then we should be thankful to God as well. When we experience hardship, then we should be patient and endure it. In times of ease and comfort, we should not become proud of what we have; in times of adversity, we should not become despondent and fall into depression. If we keep in mind that we really do not know which condition is best for us, then it will be easier for us to go through the ups and downs of life. At times, going through some difficulty is best for us even though we might not comprehend it at that time. Many people have achieved success because the hardships of life made them into stronger individuals.

84. Prophet Muhammed ﷺ said, "Do not look to those above you. Look to those below you, as it will more likely remind you of God's favors bestowed on you." [Bukhari]

Commentary: The Prophet of Mercy reminds us that we should be happy with whatever we have and we should not look with a jealous gaze towards those who have it better. When we look at those who have more than us, then we will never be happy with our state and condition. But when we look at those who have less than us, not for the purpose of belittling them, but rather for the purpose of being happy with what we have, then we will experience joy and happiness in our lives. Today, many people are deprived from the joys of life because their eyes are constantly on the rich and famous and hence, because they are not like them, they are in a constant state of grief and sorrow.

85. Prophet Muhammed ﷺ said, "Simplicity is a part of religion. Simplicity is a part of religion." [Abu Dawood]

Commentary: The Prophet of Mercy strongly emphasized the concept of simplicity through his words and actions. Today, we live in an era where we are enticed to buy things even though we do not have the money on hand to buy those things. With mortgages and credit, we buy things with money that we do not have, to please people who might not like us. Let us try our utmost to live a life of simplicity with respect to our houses, vehicles and clothes and a host of other things. If we don't have the money on hand to buy something, why fall into debt? If we live a life of simplicity then we will never become bankrupt. A person who takes the middle path in spending will not have to experience the pangs of poverty. Will Smith says, "Too many people spend money they haven't earned, to buy things they don't want, to impress people they don't like."

This hadith means more than just being simple in material things. It is emphasizing simplicity IN religion as well. So many people make religion more complicated than it needs to be.

86. Prophet Muhammed ﷺ said, "There are two blessings in which most people incur a loss: Good health and free time." [Bukhari]

Commentary: We all have many blessings which we enjoy on a daily basis. From amongst them, two important ones are good health and free time. The Prophet Muhammed ﷺ reminds us that many of us fail to utilize these two bounties in the most efficient manner and therefore, we incur a huge loss. With good health, we can achieve many things in life but our good health is often wasted in useless pursuits. We can also harm our good health by not taking care of ourselves. The same is the case with free time. Many of us do not utilize our time correctly and it goes to waste. If we utilize our health and our time efficiently, then we can benefit ourselves spiritually, physically, intellectually, and through a number of other ways. Those who achieved greatness in life learnt how to harness their time and achieved the most they could in the time they had.

87. Prophet Muhammed ﷺ said, "God loves a servant who when performing a task does so skillfully." [Bayhaqi]

Commentary: We are reminded that whatever we do in life, we should try our utmost to give it the best effort we can. If we are going to do something, we might as well try to do it 100%. We should have lofty goals and we should try to excel in everything which we do. People have become great and excelled in their professions because of the extra effort they made. We should never settle for second best and we should never be content with doing things haphazardly. Even though we cannot be perfect in everything we do, but that should not make us be lazy and lethargic when doing things. It is interesting to note that Prophet Muhammed ﷺ mentions that God **loves** a person when the person does a certain task in the most excellent manner. If we want our action to be loved by God, then we should try to do in the most perfect manner. In another narration, Prophet Muhammed ﷺ said, "Verily, God has commanded us to do everything in the most excellent manner." [Muslim]

88. Prophet Muhammed ﷺ said, "Whoever has hair, he should respect them." [Abu Dawood]

Commentary: The Prophet of Mercy did not only care about our spiritual wellbeing, but he even cared about our physical appearance as well. Here he reminds us that we must look neat and clean and we must take care of our hair by combing and cutting when necessary. Having disheveled hair and not looking neat in appearance is not a sign of piety. This advice is extremely important for husbands and wives as well that we need to make sure that we try our utmost to look physically attractive to our spouses.

89. Prophet Muhammed ﷺ said, "Whoever does you a favor, repay him, and if you are unable to, then at least pray for him." [Tabarani]

Commentary: Throughout our lives, many people have helped us and continue to assist us. When someone helps us out, we should repay that assistance. If we are not able to repay that favor by paying the person, then we should at least mention some good words by either praying for the person or by saying thank you. Even though we help others without any ulterior motives, we would think twice before helping out the same person in the future if he did not even have the manners to thank us. Though we should not hold someone's bad manners against them, it is not easy to help the ungrateful person.

90. Prophet Muhammed ﷺ said, "Cleanliness is half of faith." [Muslim]

Commentary: Our bodies, clothes, books, classrooms, homes, yards, vehicles, pathways etc. must be kept clean and tidy at all times. It is interesting that even though this pertinent advice was given over 1,400 years ago, we human beings still have not truly implemented it in our lives.

91. Prophet Muhammed ﷺ said, "Never drink wine." [Ahmad]

Commentary: Only three words are mentioned in the above statement but they are deep in meaning. The long-term spiritual, physical, financial, mental, social, and psychological harms of alcoholism have been extensively documented. Many say and do things while drunk which they regret for the rest of their lives, particularly violent and criminal acts that land them in jail. In the US, an average of one alcohol-impaired-driving fatality occurred every 48 minutes in 2009. [http://www-nrd.nhtsa.dot.gov/Pubs/811385.PDF]

Some of the adverse health effects of excessive alcohol consumption include damage to the brain, liver, pancreas, stomach, small intestine and central nervous system. Many doctors have discussed the benefits of alcohol, particularly wine. Prophet Muhammed ﷺ knew of and acknowledged that there may be benefits to the consumption of alcohol in trace amounts. However, in God's infinite wisdom, God decreed that what is harmful to such an extent in large amounts should also be avoided in small amounts. Under certain guidelines, Muslims are permitted to consume medicine which has traces of alcohol in it.

92. Prophet Muhammed ﷺ said, "When you visit a sick person, reassure him that he is going to live, because although that does not change anything, it will comfort him and lift up his spirits." [Tirmidhi]

Commentary: The Prophet of Mercy teaches us some etiquettes of visiting the sick. We should say things to give the sick person hope and make them happy. A kind word in such a situation is appreciated, for that will provide some comfort the sick person. Let us ask: When was the last time we visited a sick person at their home or at the hospital? If we were sick, wouldn't we appreciate it if someone visited us? If we cannot visit, then at a minimum, we should call and give verbal support to the person.

Financial Transactions

93. Prophet Muhammed ﷺ said "Pay the laborer his wages before his sweat dries." [Ibn Majah]

Commentary: The Prophet of Mercy understood the value of hard labor and he reminds us that we should not abuse workers. The kind thing to do is to pay the laborer even before he finishes the job. When the job is just about to be completed, to pay the laborer at that time is in accordance to the highest of manners. To pay the laborer after the work is completed is doing justice and being fair. To not pay the laborer at all or to delay the payment is oppression. Just because someone cannot find a job somewhere else, that does not mean that we should abuse the laborer by not paying him or her on time. If we cannot pay the worker on time, we should inform the employee that they can go and work somewhere else if they want to because you cannot guarantee their wages on a timely basis. We like to be paid on time; similarly, we should not delay in paying other people their wages.

94. Prophet Muhammed ﷺ said, "A truthful and trustworthy merchant is associated with the prophets." [Tirmidhi]

Commentary: Honesty in all business transactions is emphasized and Prophet Muhammed ﷺ exhorts all of us to be honest in all of our dealings. Sadly, today those two extremely important qualities of telling the truth and being a trustworthy businessman is rapidly disappearing from society. With the desire of 'making a quick buck' there is widespread deceit all around us. So many businesses lie and cheat their customers and it is becoming extremely difficult for a customer to find honest businessmen in the service industry. One mechanic quotes a price for $600 and for the same work another does it for $200. People lose faith and become wary after dealing with such situations on a regular basis. Being truthful is imperative for a society to be prosperous and sustainable. Lying is one of the major elements of corruption in human society, and the cause of the destruction of social structure and ties. When an environment of honesty and trustworthiness permeates a society, everybody benefits and when an environment of dishonesty and deceitfulness engulfs a society, everyone is robbed of their sense of peace and comfort.

95. Prophet Muhammed ﷺ said "It is better for anyone of you to take his rope and to go to the mountain and bring a bundle of wood on his back, sell it and cover his needs, than to ask people, either they give him or refuse." [Bukhari]

Commentary: The Prophet of Mercy reminds all of us that we should not be stretching out our hands and begging from people. We need to make every effort possible to take up whichever occupation we can to earn our own livelihood. If that means that we have to take up the most menial of jobs, then we should in the interest of not living off other people's money. How can people still in their young age not work on their own and expect other people to look after them? Accepting the lowest paying jobs is much better than begging or continuously living off the government and people's taxes.

This is not to say that the Prophet did not believe in social security or the bolstering of society with social services. It is simply to state that the Prophet wanted able-bodied and able-minded people to make every effort to make a living for themselves. This instills self-reliance, self-esteem and confidence in the people and makes them self-sufficient. When the people do fall on genuinely hard times, it is then that the community should come together to help.

96 Prophet Muhammed ﷺ said, "Beware of greed. It destroyed those before you. They shed one another's blood and broke off relations with their relatives." [Bukhari in AM]

Commentary: A whole book can be written on the above statement. Today, we break off relationships with others because of greed. We lie about others because of greed. We injure others because of greed. We have shed streams of the blood of the innocent and we continue to do so, because of unbridled greed. We have perpetrated heinous acts against humanity because of rampant greed. We have put countless human beings in endless misery and we have done such acts against humanity that have made countless people mourn and weep. In the name of power, wealth, position, oil, land, and natural resources, we have hurt others. Humanity! Let us take a deep breath, step back and ask ourselves, to what extent will we hurt others for worldly gain?

97. Prophet Muhammed ﷺ said, "Anybody who believes in God and the Last Day should not harm his neighbor, and anybody who believes in God and the Last Day should entertain his guest generously, and anybody who believes in God and the Last Day should talk what is good or keep quiet." [Bukhari]

Commentary: The above statement advises us that if we consider ourselves to be pious and of sound character, then we should not harm our neighbor and we should treat our guests generously and we should only speak those things in which there is some good in it or we should remain silent. Such simple words were uttered 1,400 years ago but they are still relevant today as they were then! We even have developed modern maxims like the Golden Rule and the saying, "If you don't have anything nice to say, don't say anything at all" to encapsulate the ideas espoused by the Prophet. These are universal ideas for how a thriving society should operate and how people should try to interact with one another.

98. "Prophet Muhammed ﷺ denounced the bribing person and the one who accepts the bribe." [Abu Dawood]

Commentary: Numerous cases of bribery are regularly reported in politics and business. Today giving bribes and accepting bribes has become rampant in society. The rich are involved in bribery as well as the poor. The first world countries are steeped in this as well as the third world countries. In developing countries, people can hardly get anything done without giving bribes. In the developed countries, we give it different names, such as "campaign contributions," or funding from "interest groups." But the end result is the same: The local average person loses out because big money works to the detriment of the average person. Directors and mangers of multi-national firms have been fined repeatedly for offering bribes to workers and politicians to win business. Many former commissioners and politicians have been found guilty of corruption for accepting bribes to see projects through or advance an agenda at the detriment of the general public.

Again, the Prophet warns against bribing and accepting bribes because he understood how detrimental it would be to the psyche of a community. Bribery robs society of its foundational trust. It strips officials of their trustworthiness and leaves them and the system they work for bare for people to either join in on the abuse or become so disenchanted or overwhelmed that they either disengage from society or they take the "if you can't beat them, join them" attitude and become corrupted themselves.

Gender Relations

99. Prophet Muhammed ﷺ said, "When promiscuous behavior becomes rampant in a nation, God will send upon them such (strange) diseases that their own ancestors never heard of." [Tabarani]

Commentary: The Prophet of Mercy informed all of humanity more than 1,400 years ago about the negative consequences of promiscuity. In modern times, we have witnessed the spread of sexually transmitted diseases and illnesses that did not exist in ancient times. Humanity! A few moments of pleasure should not be at the expense of a lifetime of pain. God can forgive us for being immoral, but biology at times will not forgive us if we become afflicted with a sexually transmitted infection.

100. Prophet Muhammed ﷺ said, "No man is alone with a marriageable woman but the devil is the third one present." [Tirmidhi]

Commentary: The Prophet of Mercy reminds us about the harms of being alone with the opposite gender. Many rich and famous people have lost all respect in society because of illicit relationships. The above teaching advises us that when a man is alone with another woman, that could be a recipe for being unfaithful. It doesn't matter how pious and righteous and faithful we are, as soon as we are alone with the opposite gender, we could start getting thoughts about doing something immoral with the person. The best way to prevent ourselves is to make sure that we are not alone with the opposite gender. Many marriages have been shattered because of the husband and wife being unfaithful to each other. The first step to that wrong action was by being alone with the opposite gender. For further information on this topic, please contact Kobe Bryant or Tiger Woods or David Beckham. Unfortunately, two of the three mentioned athlete's marriages have ended in divorce. The noble values promulgated by Islam 1,400 years ago, if implemented, can bring so much tranquility and serenity in our society.

What non-Muslims wrote about Prophet Muhammed ﷺ

"My choice of Muhammad to lead the list of the world's most influential persons may surprise some readers and may be questioned by others, but he was the only man in history who was supremely successful on both the religious and secular level."

[Michael H. Hart, THE 100: A RANKING OF THE MOST INFLUENTIAL PERSONS IN HISTORY, *New York: Hart Publishing Company, Inc., 1978, p. 33.*]

"He was Caesar and Pope in one; but he was Pope without Pope's pretensions, Caesar without the legions of Caesar: without a standing army, without a bodyguard, without a palace, without a fixed revenue. If ever any man had the right to say that he ruled by the right divine, it was Mohammad, for he had all the power without its instruments and without its supports."

[Bosworth Smith, MOHAMMAD AND MOHAMMADANISM, *London 1874, p. 92.*]

"It is not the propagation but the permanency of his religion that deserves our wonder; the same pure and perfect impression which he engraved at Mecca and Madina is preserved, after the revolutions of twelve centuries by the Indian, the African and the Turkish proselytes of the Koran... The Mahometans have uniformly withstood the temptation of reducing the object of their faith and devotion to a level with the senses and imagination of man. I believe in One God and Mahomet is the Apostle of God' is the simple and invariable profession of Islam. The intellectual image of the Deity has never been degraded by any visible idol; the honors of the prophet have never transgressed the measure of human virtue; and his living precepts have restrained the gratitude of his disciples within the bounds of reason and religion."

[**Edward Gibbon and Simon Ocklay,** HISTORY OF THE SARACEN EMPIRE, *London, 1870, p. 54.*]

"It is impossible for anyone who studies the life and character of the great Prophet of Arabia, who knows how he taught and how he lived, to feel anything but reverence for that mighty Prophet, one of the great messengers of the Supreme. And although in what I put to you I shall say many things which may be familiar to many, yet I myself feel whenever I re-read them, a new way of admiration, a new sense of reverence for that mighty Arabian teacher."

[**Annie Besant,** THE LIFE AND TEACHINGS OF MUHAMMAD, *Madras, 1932, p. 4.*]

"His readiness to undergo persecution for his beliefs, the high moral character of the men who believed in him and looked up to him as leader, and the greatness of his ultimate achievement all argue his fundamental integrity. To suppose Muhammad an impostor raises more problems than it solves. Moreover, none of the great figures of history is so poorly appreciated in the West as Muhammad."

[**W Montgomery Watt,** MOHAMMAD AT MECCA, *Oxford, 1953, p. 52.*]

"Philosopher, orator, apostle, legislator, warrior, conqueror of ideas, restorer of rational dogmas, of a cult without images; the founder of twenty terrestrial empires and of one spiritual empire, that is Muhammad. As regards all standards by which human greatness may be measured, we may well ask, is there any man greater than he?"

[**Lamartine,** HISTOIRE DE LA TURQUIE, *Paris, 1854, Vol. II, pp. 276-277.*]

"He must be called the Savior of Humanity. I believe that if a man like him were to assume the dictatorship of the modern world, he would succeed in solving its problems in a way that would bring it much needed peace and happiness."

[**George Bernard Shaw,** THE GENUINE ISLAM, *Singapore, Vol. 1, No. 8, 1936*]

"I wanted to know the best of one who holds today undisputed sway over the hearts of millions of mankind... I became more than convinced that it was not the sword that won a place for Islam in those days in the scheme of life. It was the rigid simplicity, the utter self-effacement of the Prophet, the scrupulous regard for his pledges, his intense devotion to his friends and followers, his intrepidity, his fearlessness, his absolute trust in God and in his own mission. These and not the sword carried everything before them and surmounted every obstacle. When I closed the 2nd volume (of the Prophet's biography), I was sorry there was not more for me to read of the great life."

[**Mahatma Gandhi (1869-1948),** *in a 1924 publication of "Young India"*]

Suggestions For Further Reading

ARMSTRONG, Karen,
Muhammad: A Biography of the Prophet

LINGS, Martin,
Muhammad: His Life Based on the Earliest Sources

AHMED, Akbar,
Islam Today: A Short Introduction to the Muslim World

YUSUF, Hamza,
The Content of Character—Ethical Sayings of Prophet Muhammad

ESPOSITO, John,
The Oxford History of Islam

NADWI, Sulaiman,
Muhammad: The Ideal Prophet

SHEIKH, Zia,
Islam: Silencing the Critics

WATT, W Montgomery,
Muhammad at Mecca

WATT, W Montgomery,
Muhammad at Medina

KABAH, MAKKAH, SAUDI ARABIA

PROPHET'S MOSQUE, MADINAH, SAUDI ARABIA

DOME OF THE ROCK, JERUSALEM

UMAYYAD MOSQUE, DAMASCUS, SYRIA

SHEIKH ZAYED MOSQUE, ABU DHABI, U.A.E.

JAME MASJID, DELHI, INDIA

MUHAMMED ALI MOSQUE, CAIRO, EGYPT

KING FAISAL MOSQUE, ISLAMABAD, PAKISTAN

IMAM ABDUL WAHHAB MOSQUE, DOHA, QATAR

KUL SHARIF MOSQUE, KAZAN KREMLIN, RUSSIA